# A, B
# and M

## Road Numbering Revealed

Andrew Emmerson
and
Peter Bancroft

CAPITAL HISTORY

*Dedicated to the memory of Peter Bancroft: meticulous researcher, true professional and very good friend.*

**Other books by the writers**

Peter Bancroft:
- *British Transport Staff College at Woking*
- *London Transport Records at the Public Record Office*
- *Railways Around Alton: An Illustrated Bibliography*
- *The Railway to King William Street and Southwark Deep Tunnel Air-Raid Shelter.*

Andrew Emmerson:
- *Electronic Classics*
- *London's Secret Tubes*
- *Old Telephones*
- *Old Television*
- *The Underground Pioneers.*

First published 2007

ISBN 978-185414-307-5

Published by Capital History, PO Box 250, Harrow, HA3 5ZH

Printed by Thomson Press, Lyon Road, Harrow, HA1 2AG.

*Front cover map: Mike Harris*

# CONTENTS

INTRODUCTION
An arcane subject: the joy of numbers 6

1. EARLY TIMES
   When roads had names, not numbers 8

2. THE TURNPIKE ERA
   Strategic road improvement begins 14

3. THE TWENTIETH CENTURY
   Road numbers become established 18

4. THE MOTORWAY ERA
   A new layer of complexity 47

5. CAPITAL HIGHWAYS
   The streets of London: a special case 60

6. NUMBERS THAT DON'T ADD UP
   Missing numbers, misplaced roads and other oddities 66

7. BRITAIN'S OTHER NUMBERED ROADS
   Milton Keynes, Euroroutes and other odd numbers 73

8. ISLANDS AND IRELAND
   Trunks, Links and other exotic delights 80

TERMS USED IN THIS BOOK 90

FURTHER READING 92

INDEX 94

# PREFACE

Simple questions can sometimes be hard to answer. For instance, who devised Britain's road numbers and when? Plenty of writers have analysed the mechanics of numbering, yet until now none of the books, articles and websites has actually set out the origin of the scheme, its timing or the motivation for classifying our roads.

Peter Bancroft wanted to know and he was determined to find out. After searching through books and questioning government departments and other authorities in vain, he realised the only way he would find out was by consulting the original papers in the National Archives and elsewhere.

So began a fascinating journey of discovery that took several years to complete and culminated in the book you are reading now. Sadly, Peter never came to see his studies turned into print and it was a cruel twist of fate that took his life before he could finish his work. Fortunately he left comprehensive notes and records, enabling me to complete and expand his text to become the definitive study for now of this fascinatingly obscure topic. His meticulous historical research serves as its own memorial.

The book could not have been produced without the help and support of Peter's brother, David Bancroft and several of his friends including Mike Horne, George Jasieniecki, Chris Larsen, John Liffen, John Parkin and Jonathan Roberts, who provided valuable information and photographs. Photos and maps provided by Collins Bartholomew, Getty Images, Chris Larsen, John Parkin, Peterborough Museum and the RAC. Thanks go also to Stan Basnett (Isle of Man), Bob Cookson, Chris Lawson (Royal Automobile Club), Donald MacRae (Western Isles Council), Chris Marshall, Rodney Marshall, David St George (Public Services Committee, States of Jersey), Iain Simmons (Local Transportation Planning Manager, Corporation of London); Peter Tidd (States of Guernsey), Melanie Todd (Collins Bartholomew), Glenys Wass (Peterborough Museum and Art Gallery) and Les Wilson (Isle of Man). An enthusiastic tip of the cap goes also to the Sabristi – members of the Society for All British Road Enthusiasts.

Andrew Emmerson

# INTRODUCTION

Not long ago the BBC website offered this innocuous advice to its readers:

> "In connection with this weekend's British Grand Prix at Silverstone, southbound traffic wishing to avoid congestion in the area should use the C54 between the A5 Litchborough turn to Banbury and the M40."

Doubtless based on official information and intended to be helpful, it would have meant precisely nothing to the average motorist, who would search in vain for the C54 on maps or direction signs. But for 'roaders', the intrepid band of enthusiasts devoted to studying road lore and numbering knowledge, this mention of the C54 was one of those fortunate slips that occasionally shed light on an otherwise undisclosed world.

This is indeed the joy of numbers. For although you might think nothing could be more prosaic than road numbers, the commonplace notations such as A1, B4525 and M25 are only the tip of a largely uncharted realm of road numbering. Unknown to the public at large, there are 'C' roads, 'E' roads and 'U' roads as well as some shadowy numbering schemes known only to a select few. Roads have been renumbered, motorways have been reclassified as 'A' roads and gaps left in numbering schemes for new-build projects that were never realised. Plans exist as far back as 1906 for might-have-been motorways, whilst concrete evidence is visible to those with keen eyes for grandiose road building projects that were started but never completed.

Enquiring minds will wonder if there are other numbering anomalies and why so many road numbers are never shown on maps or signs. They will want to know who devised Britain's road numbering scheme, when and for what purpose. They may even be curious to know a little more about the history of our highways, byways and motorways, not only in Great Britain but also the Irish Republic.

Information on these fascinating subjects is generally hard to find. Discussion groups exist on the Internet but until now there has been no comprehensive survey in book form. This book sets out to correct this deficiency.

The United Kingdom is today a country crowded with cars, buses and lorries, struggling to travel a trunk road system that dates back in some places to the 1st century AD. By the third century numbers had already been allocated to some of these routes, arguably the first road numbers in the British Isles.

Systematic management of Britain's road network began with the Romans. Mileposts, such as this one from Chesterton near Peterborough, as well as numbered routes are all part of the Roman legacy. The inscription on this milestone, dedicated to Emperor Victorinus, dates it to a time between 268 and 270 AD (the actual year has been defaced).

For that reason, although it was only in 1914 that work first started on the current system of classifying and numbering the nation's highways, it seemed logical to go back to the beginnings of transportation and to remind ourselves of the significance of some of the early trackways and later Roman roads. Some of these trackways and roads have names that remain with us in one form or another, and are still shown on maps some two thousand years later.

To put all this into context the book also examines the overall evolution of the road network, and early attempts at maintenance and improvement. Finally for the sake of completeness, we cover the separate road classification systems in Northern Ireland, the Republic of Ireland and the various island groups around the United Kingdom.

# 1
# EARLY TIMES
## When roads had names, not numbers

Understandably we take for granted the road network, its maintenance and improvement (however slow!) and the system of road numbers that appear on many maps and direction signs, to aid our getting from one place to another. Discovering how this national road numbering system developed was the starting point for this study. But having arrived at the point in 1914 when work on the classification and resulting numbering scheme first began, it seemed pertinent to look back further … .

It is worth pausing a moment and considering why roads might need numbers. Road numbers serve two functions, to help travellers to plan routes and find their way, also to assist administrators who needed to keep records at remote locations.

## Ancient trackways and Roman roads

On that basis it is immediately obvious that our ancient forefathers had little need of road numbers. Most people did not travel far and those who did would take a guide if they were unfamiliar with the way. In either case, names were far more important than numbers. Many of the important trackways and ridgeways dating from ancient time have names, although the names themselves date probably from more recent times. Their original names are largely forgotten, along with the names tagged locally to the vast number of other tracks and paths. Some of the better known names ascribed to them today are shown below.

| Name: | Approximate start: | Approximate finish: |
|---|---|---|
| Ashwell Street | Ashwell | North of Royston |
| Harrow Way (or Hoar Way) | Stonehenge | Folkestone |
| High Street | Horncastle/Caistor | The Humber at South Ferriby |
| Icknield Way | North-east of Newmarket | Near Uffington White Horse |
| Jurassic Way (largely super-seded by Fosse Way) | The Humber | The Severn |
| Middle Street | Lincoln | The Humber |
| Pilgrims' Way (duplicates part of Harrow Way) | Winchester | Canterbury |
| Sewstern Lane | Stamford area | The Trent at Newark |

Many of these ancient trackways were used largely by travellers on foot or horseback, which enabled them to keep to the high ground away from winter flooding and where the absence of trees made ambush less likely. These routes were not defined as closely as today's roads, making it easy to avoid boggy patches and other obstacles. For subsequent roadways these routes were less suitable. They did not always pass close to population centres, nor did the steep slopes involved at some places make easy passage for the wheeled vehicles used later on. This situation changed dramatically after the Romans invaded and occupied this country.

During the Roman occupation of Britain from the first invasion in 43AD to the final withdrawal in 410AD, many new (and direct) roads were built. These were designed principally to link their cities and military stations. Some roads included milestones, which also date from the Roman period. The main Roman roads, along with the names given to them today (dating in fact mostly from much later periods), are shown below:

| Name: | Approx start: | Approximate finish: | Course followed in part by present 'A' and 'B' roads: |
|---|---|---|---|
| Akeman Street | Cirencester | St Albans | A41 |
| Dere Street | North-east of York | St Boswells | A1167/A1/B6275/B6286/A691/B6309/A68 (parts) |
| Ermin Way | Cirencester | Gloucester | A417 |
| Ermine Street | London | Lincoln (and on towards Humber Estuary) | A10/A14/A1/B6403/A15/B1207 |
| Fosse (or Foss) Way | Exeter | Lincoln | A30/A303/A37/A433/A429/B4029/A46 |
| King Street | West of | Towards Lincoln | Short section of B1443 |
| Peddars Way | Holme next the Sea | Stane Street (near Colchester) | |
| Ryknield (also Ryknild or Riknild) Street | Bourton | Chesterfield | B4009/B489 |
| Sarre Wall | Thanet | Canterbury | A28 |
| Stanegate | Greenhead | Corbridge | Part is closely parallel to the B6318 |
| Stane Street | Braughing | Colchester | A120/A12 |
| Stane Street | Chichester | London | A285/A29 |
| Stone Street | Lympne | Canterbury | B2068 |
| Via Devana | Gog Magog Hills (south-east of Cambridge) | Leicester | A604 |

| Name: | Approx start: | Approximate finish: | Course followed in part by present 'A' and 'B' roads: |
|---|---|---|---|
| Vicinal Way (also Ealde Street) | London (Aldgate) | Eastwards along present A11 via Mile End Road and eventually to Colchester | Part of A11 and A12 |
| Watling Street | Dover | Wroxeter | A2/A207/A5 |

Large sections of these principal Roman routes are still followed by present-day motor roads.

Central administration of roads came with the Romans and then largely for military purposes, enabling commanders to calculate how long it would take troops to march from one garrison to another. Whether the Roman roads were themselves numbered is a matter for discussion but what is not in dispute is that Antoninus Augustus produced a gazetteer of recommended routes, in which the British section *Iter Britanniarvm [The British Routes]* surveyed 15 different journeys. We could argue that this survey was Britain's first road numbering scheme (the identification of some of the Roman sites is still uncertain):

| Journey no.: | Start: | Finish: |
|---|---|---|
| I | BREMENIUM = High Rochester, Northumberland | PRAESIDIUM = Bridlington, Humberside |
| II | BLATOBULGIUM = Birrens, Dumfries & Galloway | RUTUPIAE = Richborough, Kent |
| III | LONDINIUM = London | PORTUS DUBRIS = Dover, Kent |
| IV | LONDINIUM = London | PORTUS LEMANIS = Lympne, Kent |
| V | LONDINIUM = London | LUGUVALLIUM = Carlisle, Cumbria |
| VI | LONDINIUM = London | LINDUM = Lincoln, Lincolnshire |
| VII | REGNORUM = Chichester, Sussex | LONDINIUM = London |
| VIII | EBURACUM = York | LONDINIUM = London |
| IX | VENTA ICINORUM = Caistor St. Edmund, Norfolk | LONDINIUM = London |
| X | GLANNOVENTA = Ravenglass, Cumbria | MEDIOLANUM = Whitchurch, Shropshire |
| XI | SEGONTIUM = Caernarfon, Gwynedd | DEVA = Chester |
| XII | MORIDUNUM = Carmarthen, Dyfed | VIROCONIUM = Wroxeter, Shropshire |
| XIII | ISCA SILURUM = Caerleon, Gwent | CALLEVA ATREBATUM = Silchester, Hampshire |
| XIV | As XIII (alternative route) | |
| XV | CALLEVA ATREBATUM = Silchester, Hampshire | ISCA = Exeter, Devon |

Strange to say, it is not entirely clear who Antoninus Augustus actually was. Nor are his itineraries all of one date, although most seem to be from the third century. Other Roman roads in Britain have numbers but these have been allocated by 20th century scholars. Names given to Roman roads, such as Watling Street, are of Anglo-Saxon origin, not Roman. Latin road names shown in medieval records (for example Via Regia, the King's Highway) are also not of Roman origin.

## Middle Ages

The Anglo-Saxon raids of the fourth century caused the destruction of many Roman villas and led to the decay of their towns and roads, and the breakdown of what centralised administration there had been in the Roman period. Road building and maintenance as such came to a complete halt, and many of the existing roads seem to have been broken up. However, their routes have often remained, as many modern roads follow the alignment of the earlier Roman roads, traversing long straight courses across the countryside.

By the Middle Ages, the church had assumed responsibility for some road repair and maintenance and the building of a great many bridges. The richer monasteries took the lead and even some religious guilds were formed, with bishops granting indulgences to those who contributed money and labour. Thus, some bridges even had chapels built on them. (One of the earliest examples was the bridge built at Elvet Bridge in Durham in 1174, which had a chapel at either end.) Also a special clause was inserted in the Litany for the safety of travellers. This was an acknowledgement that bands of robbers often lurked in the undergrowth at the roadside. It was this ever present problem that eventually inspired the State to take action.

## State intervention

The true beginning of highway legislation in this country goes back some 718 years to the reign of Edward I. On the Eighth of October in the thirteenth year of his reign, A.D.1285, the Statute of Winchester was passed. This covered various matters, but included the following words relating to highways:

'AND Further, It is commanded, That Highways leading from one Market Town to another shall be enlarged, whereas (Bushes Woods) or Dykes be, so that there be neither Dyke (Tree) nor Bush, whereby a Man may lurk to do hurt, within two hundred foot of the one side, and two hundred foot on the other side of the way, so that this Statute shall not extend unto (Ashes) nor unto great Trees, (for which it shall be clearly out of this.) And if by Default of the Lord that will not abate the Dyke, Underwood or Bushes, in the manner aforesaid, any Robberies be done therein, the Lord shall be answerable for the felony; and if murther be done the Lord shall make a Fine at the King's Pleasure. And if the Lord be not able to fell the Underwoods, the Country shall aid him therein. And the King willeth, that in his demean Lands and Woods within his Forest and without, the Ways shall be enlarged, as before said. And if percase a Park be (taken from) the Highway, it is requisite that the Lord shall (set) his Park (the space of two hundred foot from the Highways) as before is said, or that he make such a Wall, Dyke, or Hedge, that Offenders may not pass, nor return to do evil.'

It remains to be seen if this legislation was ever enforced.

## From Tudor times

When the monasteries were dissolved by Henry VIII later in his reign, one of the principal landowners was swept away, together with its haphazard system of road maintenance. The monks, one of the chief classes of traveller, were also removed. The public soon clamoured for improvements however and Parliament now intervened more decisively. This next important piece of legislation relating to roads was The Highways Act of 1555, its actual title being 'An Acte for tha mendyng of Highe Wayes'. From this time, the parishes were responsible for the upkeep of the roads that passed through their areas. The local Constables and Churchwardens in every parish met once a year on the Tuesday or Wednesday of Easter week and elected two honest persons to be surveyors and orderers for one year. They would also name and appoint four days during which the local inhabitants would mend the roads. This work had to take place before the feast of the Nativity of St John Baptist following. This compulsory labour to repair the roads was to be supplemented by local farmers supplying carts and materials. All parishioners were to contribute in some way, and the surveyor appointed to oversee this work could extract fines for the many offences that this statute created. This Act was to be in force only for seven years. However, little seems to have been achieved in this way.

In 1562–3, a further Act was passed that extended the 1555 Act for a further 20 years and introduced a number of smaller changes. Also under the new Act, gravel could now be dug without the need for permission. More significantly to the local inhabitants, there was also a change to the number of days during which the roads had to be mended, this now being increased from four to six. It was also required that ditches, hedges, fences and trees should be scoured, kept low and lopped as necessary.

In 1577, William Harrison published his *Description of England*, which included information about the 'common ways' between towns and gave details of the distances involved. This information was no doubt helpful for people planning journeys. Similar itineraries of England were published by John Leland between 1533 and 1539 and maps had also started to appear on the market, such as those of Christopher Caxton, who undertook a survey of all the counties in England and Wales about this time. Post-horses had also appeared and from 1572, a postal service (for official use only) was offered between a list of prescribed places.

In 1584–5, a further Act was passed that continued the 1555 Act until the end of that Session. It was made perpetual shortly after by another Act. (It remained in force until 1835.)

In 1662, 'An Act for enlarging and repairing of common High wayes', was passed. This included power to levy rates and for the surveyors to hire labourers and carts using the money so collected. Power was also given to take adjoining lands to widen the roads if they were less than eight yards wide, eight yards being considered the standard width. Power to dig gravel from neighbouring commons without payment was also given, together with power to dig gravel from private grounds with the exception of orchards, courtyards, parks containing deer or meadows. This Act also restricted the weight of goods that could be carried for hire and stipulated the maximum number of horses, etc. that could be used to pull carts. No tyres were to be less than four inches in breadth. Bridges were to have sufficient walls or posts and rails. It was now made the case that if land was rented out to a tenant, then the tenant and not the landlord was responsible for the payment of any rate assessment. This Act was to be in force only until the end of the first Session of the next Parliament, with the power to raise money continuing for three years.

# 2
# THE TURNPIKE ERA
## Strategic road improvement begins

## The Turnpike Acts

In 1663, the first Turnpike Act was passed. Its full title was, 'An Act for repairing the Highwayes within the Countyes of Hertford Cambridge and Huntington'. The Act stated that the ordinary course was not sufficient for the effective repair of roads due to high traffic levels, for which reason four Justices for each of the said counties were empowered to appoint nine surveyors who would act in their own county only. The surveyors would consider and direct any repairs necessary and also appoint people to act as toll gatherers.

The rates set out in the Act applied 'for every Horse one penny, for every Coach six pence, for every Waggon one shilling, for every Cart eight pence, for every score of Sheepe or Lambes one (halfe) penny', and so on, with three fixed toll-collecting places to be established in each county. In this way the cost of maintaining roads passed from the parishioners to a proportion of the road users themselves.

Further Acts followed although the idea of turnpiking sections of road generally was slow to catch on. In part this was due to some resistance to tolls until the resulting improvements were more widely recognised. This same period saw the publication of Road Books, an updated version of the Antonine Itineraries of Roman times. The first truly comprehensive road book was produced by Ogilvy in 1675 and derivatives continued to be published well into the 20th century. Probably their last apparition was the orange-covered route sheets issued to Automobile Association members on request.

Another far-reaching piece of legislation, passed in the Session 1696–7, 'An Act for enlargeing Common High-ways', empowered local Quarter Sessions to enlarge highways by taking up to eight yards in width but not to pull down any houses. It also included powers to erect a stone or post at places where highways crossed or met, to show the next market town to which each of the said joining highways lead. This is the first instance of signage being mentioned in legislation.

Fingerposts and milestones date back many centuries but it was not until 1696–7 that local authorities were given specific powers to erect them at public expense.

## Private involvement

A major development occurred in 1706 when Parliament created the first true Turnpike Trust under the 'Act for repairing the Highway between Fornhill in the County of Bedford and the Town of Stony Stratford in the County of Buckingham'. Whereas previous legislation had put road improvement in the hands of public authorities, this Act created a private-public partnership by naming 32 trustees (all gentlemen) who were given power to, 'erect Gate or Gates Turnpike or Turnpikes cross any Part or Parts of the said Road'. They would also receive and take the tolls set out in the Act and spend the money on repairing the roads, with permission to borrow money at six per cent per annum. In effect, the local gentry now took over from the parish the particular length of road named in the Act.

By 1750, there were about 400 such Toll Trusts, some of them overseeing relatively short stretches of the main roads. Local people were at first hostile to these Toll Trusts, because it meant that they had to pay to use what were in effect their local roads. Similarly, there was a feeling that the roads were also being up-kept for the use of strangers, with riots breaking out in some areas.

Road tolling nevertheless brought real improvement to the quality of the roads affected. The number of trusts continued to rise in the second half of the 18th century and by 1830 there were 2,450. Coachbuilding for stage passenger services also started in this period, becoming an important industry. Road building and road surfacing also improved during this period influenced by important engineers such as John Metcalf, John Telford and John Loudon Macadam.

The growth of commerce and the improved state of the turnpike roads enabled commercial carriers to offer regular services by the early 19th century. This 'Canterbury and Dover common stage waggon' is depicted at its London depot at the Talbot Inn, Borough. A large number of stage wagons began from the numerous inn yards here in Southwark, a few remaining well into the 20th century as railway parcels depots (which is how the London's last galleried coaching inn, the George, survived).

## Scotland and Wales

In Scotland, an Act of the Scottish Parliament had been passed in 1669 that required Sheriffs and Justices to make lists of the roads within their bounds. They were to appoint overseers who would make, 'tennants, cottars and their servants' repair the roads, with punishment for absentees. Powers were also given to the Privy Council to order tolls to be levied.

Following the Act of Union of 1707, under which Scotland was united with England and Wales, there was soon a need to construct roads for military purposes. This was especially necessary in the Highlands, where existing communications did not favour the rapid movement of troops. The first Jacobite rising of 1715 was soon put down but its legacy was the construction of about 250 miles of relatively straight strategic roads as a precaution against further Jacobite insurrection (which arose again in 1745–6). From 1724 to 1730 General George Wade, an English General and a military engineer, constructed Scotland's first metalled roads as well as some 40 stone bridges to carry them over rivers and ravines. Some of the roads in the Highlands are still referred to individually as a 'Wade's Road'. An old rhyme has also survived into the modern day:

'Had you seen but these roads before they were made,
You would hold up your hands and bless General Wade.'

The first Act by the combined parliament affecting Scottish highways was passed in 1713 entitled, 'An Act for upholding and repairing the Bridges and Highways in the County of Edinburgh'. Under this, Justices of the Peace were nominated and appointed as Trustees and given the power to erect a gate or gates, turnpike or turnpikes and collect tolls. The first Scottish turnpike Acts as such followed somewhat later, in the period 1750–1770. Wales also saw the institution of 'county trusts' first introduced in Monmouthshire in 1755 and 1758, by which all county main roads were turnpiked together.

## Turnpikes abolished, public administration revived

The rise of canals and then the railways took away much of the long-distance goods traffic from the roads, whilst the favourable cost and speed of rail travel drew passengers away from the stage coaches. Road traffic became mainly local once more. In the same time frame was the Highways Act of 1835 which abolished the use of forced labour for the maintenance of parish roads, the work on parish roads being financed by the rates from then on. On turnpike roads maintenance was funded by tolls, although many of the turnpike trusts were rendered bankrupt by the loss of business. The Turnpike Acts Continuation Act of 1871 fixed terms for the abolition of many trusts, with such powers for these being returned to the local authorities.

Two developments of the 1880s have important implications for our study. The first was the Local Government Act of 1888, which set up County Councils in their present form. From now on these newly formed bodies would really dominate the administration of the main highways until the Ministry of Transport took over direct responsibility for trunk roads from 1936 onwards. The County Councils now took charge of the main roads, whilst in 1894 all the secondary roads became the responsibility of the Urban and Rural District Councils.

Far more significant (seen in hindsight) was a development in another country. This was the invention of the internal combustion engine by two Germans, Gottfried Daimler and Carl Benz. It was in 1887 that a vehicle first ran successfully with this form of power. In England, the new means of propulsion was greeted with suspicion and somewhat devalued by the Locomotives on Turnpike and Other Roads Act of 1865. More commonly known as the Red Flag Act, it required horseless carriages to travel at no more than 4 miles per hour, with a man walking in front bearing a red flag. Not long afterwards this law was repealed by the 1896 Locomotives on Highways Act; this new legislation introduced a speed limit of 14 miles per hour, lowered by the Local Government Board to 12mph.

# 3
# THE TWENTIETH CENTURY
## Road numbers become established

So long as roads were administered locally by local organisations, without any real practical or financial help from the central government it may be noted, there was no incentive or motivation for a national system of classification or numbering. But this was soon to change.

With the invention of the internal combustion engine, and the rise of the motor car, there was clearly a need to make massive improvements to the road network, however, and this could only really be done by central government, which could raise money for this specific purpose. But with the wish to give grants for road improvements and new construction, came the need to be able to identify which roads were of such importance as to deserve grants from what limited funds would be available. Just as important was the need to be able to identify particular stretches of these roads to which such grants might be applied. Added to this was the eventual realisation that if such a system of numbering were added to maps and signposts, it would be of great benefit to the motorists themselves, assisting navigation.

## The Road Board

Mr Lloyd George, then Chancellor of the Exchequer, used his April 1909 Budget to propose raising money for road improvements under the responsibility of a new central authority. The resulting Development and Road Improvements Fund Act 1909 received the Royal Assent on 3 December 1909. The Road Board itself was constituted on 13 May 1910 under Section 7 of the Act. The Board comprised five members each appointed by the Treasury, who also selected the Chairman. It was here that the Road Board's problems began. None of the members, nor the Chairman, had any real connection with roads and there was further criticism later on that the Board met infrequently, often merely rubber-stamping the policy of its Chairman.

The Road Board was also seen as slow to commit itself to granting the money it was given to spend. Road surfacing or crust improvements were the early targets, being more easily achieved, and the complications of significant realignments, widenings and new road construction were left to the post-1919 period. The only exceptions were the new Croydon By-Pass, the Lewes to Newhaven road improvement and the new bridge over the River Trent at Keadby Bridge. The Board also encouraged the promotion of the new Great West Road, but by 1914 it had only reached the stage of Bill promotion in Parliament, with further work halted by the outbreak of the First World War. The first contract for work on this scheme was placed only in February 1920, soon after the formation of the Ministry of Transport, to which the powers and duties of the Road Board had been transferred under an Act of September 1919.

## Classification ...

The then Road Board had been engaged in preparing a classification of the national road network from early in 1914, but this work was interrupted by the outbreak of World War One. Classification proposals had been received from 1,567 local authorities before the outbreak of war. In August 1914 the Board was also on the point of agreeing with all the local authorities of England and Wales for a census of traffic to be taken at various points. These points were to be defined by the Board, but the census was only carried out in a few instances. The Great War then intervened.

The following letter, which was often quoted in replies as to the origins of the classification scheme, usefully sums up what happened subsequently:

> 'As a result of a recommendation of the Departmental Committee on Local Taxation in March 1914, the Road Board decided to frame the proposed classification on such lines that it could be used as a basis for grants from the National Exchequer. The co-operation of Highway Authorities in the preparation of the proposed classification was invited and considerable progress had been made with the preliminary work of route numbering up to August 1914, when it was interrupted by the outbreak of war, and was not actively resumed until 1921, when the Minister of Transport, in exercise of his powers under the Ministry of Transport Act 1919, instituted the scheme of road classification that became effective in 1922 and is still in operation.'

> *Letter to E.C.W. French, dated 14 April 1958, from R.C. Barnard (Ministry of Transport) – Public Record Office MT128/59*

## ... and confusion

It appears that the original scheme was directed mainly towards ease of identification of stretches of road to which grants could be applied for in respect of road improvements. In 1913, the county of Kent's existing system of identifying particular roads was to allocate numbers to the main roads, much as the system that was eventually adopted. But it was proposed that each stretch of that road between main junctions or towns would have been allocated a further number in succession, shown in brackets after the main number. Thus road 259, for example, would have been progressively: 259(1); 259(2); 259(3); and so on, throughout its length. The identification of any one stretch would therefore have been an easy task.

It is not clear whether this numbering system would ever have appeared on route signs. A contemporary note indicates that on Ordnance Survey maps, main roads from London would be coloured red; roads connecting towns and urban districts would be shown blue (for roads between towns and urban districts over 10,000 population); green (for roads between towns and urban districts of between 5,000 and 10,000 population) and brown (for roads connecting towns and urban districts under 5,000 population).

By 1915, some general principles appear to have emerged and these were expressed in a 'Memorandum On Numbering Roads'. The idea of serially numbering subdivisions appears to have lost favour. The over-riding principle remained as the purpose of easy reference between the Central Department and the Local Authorities and others. However, it was already being proposed that a road should have one reference number from its commencement to its termination (the Great North Road from London to Inverness was cited as an example.) The collection of statistical information on road lengths, in particular Districts and County Boroughs, would also be needed.

Progress was slow. A Parliamentary question in the House of Commons in the summer of 1919 obtained the reply from junior Treasury minister Stanley Baldwin that he was not then in a position to say when the work of classification would be resumed and completed. But the passage of the Ministry of Ways and Communications Bill then before Parliament, would change the situation and lead to a new scheme being devised and introduced.

## Practical proposals emerge

Following the formation of the Ministry of Transport in 1919, the matter of route classification again came up. It was now even more important to set out which roads were considered to be of sufficient importance to qualify for a grant towards their upkeep. Scotland presented particular problems. If the definition of main roads, as 'inter town routes connecting towns having populations of 10,000 or more', were applied strictly to Scotland, many of the main roads in the north of Scotland, and practically all the main roads in the Highlands, would be excluded.

*The Autocar* of 4 December 1920 stated: 'It is, we think, unquestionable that a sound scheme of numbering the roads will be of great value to the motoring community, for, presumably, each principal road will retain the same number from end to end, and, if the traveller knows that he will be upon, say, road 10 from London to Holyhead, he will only have, at forks and road junctions, to look on the sign-post ahead of him for the figures 10 to assure himself that if he follows that direction he will not go astray. Similarly, with the smaller roads the numbering system should be helpful. We understand that it is the intention of the Minister to see that the numbering shall apply to all three of the categories into which public roads will eventually be divided.'

On 27 April 1921, the Michelin Tyre Co. Ltd wrote a letter to the Rt Hon Sir E.C. Geddes, Minister of Transport, under the heading of 'Road Numbering in the British Isles'. This followed a conversation between Michelin's representative, Mr J.H. Lingwood, and Colonel Richmond from the Ministry. The letter stated, 'that Mr. Andre Michelin most highly appreciates the honour you have conferred upon him in asking his advice on a subject which so deeply interests him'. Attached to the letter were four papers. The first of these, 'Classification of roads in France', included a then current French road map. This showed that the National Routes N1–N15 radiated from Paris in a clockwise direction (the N1 running from Paris to Calais and the N15 running from Paris to Dieppe), though not all, actually started from the centre of Paris – far from it. The next group of National Routes, from the N16–N24b also radiated from Paris in a clockwise direction interspersed in the areas between the previous roads, but again not all actually started from the centre of Paris. The second paper was entitled, 'List of disadvantages of the French numbering system'.

The third paper was entitled, 'Allocation of numbers to the roads in the British Isles'. This included a number of suggestions, but did include one that stated, 'The first numbers would be given to the roads leaving London in a northerly direction and then turning from left to right in the sense of the hands of a watch.' Transverse roads would be numbered from north to south. But these 'National' 'N' roads would create 24 sectors that would each be distinguished by a letter of the alphabet (excluding N). All the first class roads in that sector would be given a capital letter followed by the number. The second class roads in that sector would be given a serial number, followed by a lower case letter for that particular sector. These designations would not go beyond a sector boundary. The fourth paper was entitled, 'Short History of the Classification and numbering of the Routes Nationales in France' (the origin of the French numbering system was a Decree of 16 December 1811, revised in 1824).

Having contributed material advice to the road numbering debate, the Michelin company afterwards played its part in the public education process. Here the firm's Bibendum character shows a cloth-capped motorist the simplicity of the new scheme. The combination of Bibendum, strong blue and yellow colours plus the Cheltenham typeface all enhanced the strength of Michelin's public identity.

# Find your way
## by using
# the Road Numbers

Each road has been given a number which is shown on the sign-post arm and also on the Michelin Map.

Note, from the Michelin Map, the numbers of the roads to be followed and, at the cross-roads, take those which, according to the sign-posts, have the same numbers.

*Thus, you will be able to find your way just as easily as you do in a town, with a plan showing the names of the streets.*

# THE MINISTRY OF TRANSPORT'S
# ROAD NUMBERING SCHEME

## CLASSIFICATION

WHEN the Ministry of Transport was constituted it was decided that the whole of the road system of the country should be classified. This classification divides the roads into three categories, namely :—

**1st Class Roads.**
**2nd Class Roads.**
**Other Roads.**

Of these, the **1st Class Roads** consist of the Great Arterial Routes connecting London, and in Scotland, Edinburgh, with the large provincial towns, and these towns one with another.

The **2nd Class Roads**, which are possibly narrower and less important, but in other respects but little inferior to the "1st Class Roads," consist of roads connecting the minor towns with the 1st Class Roads, and with one another

The **3rd Class or Other Roads** constitute the remainder, and are maintained by purely local funds.

1st Class Roads are distinguished by the letter "A"; the 2nd Class Roads by the letter "B"; each road being allotted a number in addition to the letter.

## NUMBERING SCHEME

The whole of Great Britain is divided into nine sectors; the great arterial highways radiating from London, starting with the Great North Road, being numbered in a clockwise direction A1 to A6; the great arterial highways radiating from Edinburgh, being A7, A8 and A9.

These great routes are as follows :—

| | |
|---|---|
| A1—London to Edinburgh | A6—London to Carlisle |
| A2—London to Dover | A7—Edinburgh to Carlisle |
| A3—London to Portsmouth | A8—Edinburgh to Gourock |
| A4—London to Bath | A9—Edinburgh to Inverness |
| A5—London to Holyhead | |

Each road takes its initial number from the sector in which it starts, such sectors being the areas lying to the right of (or clockwise to) the adjacent arterial road; thus "A10" and "B156" start in Sector 1, that is in the area between the roads A1 and A2. An exception is the area lying between the road A2 and the estuary of the Thames, where for the sake of convenience the roads are reckoned as within Sector 2.

Roads running across more than one sector do not necessarily terminate (in regard to their numbering) in the same sector in which they begin; the road running from Birmingham to Ipswich being an example of this, since although it runs through Sectors 5, 6 and 1, it retains its original number of A45.

## ROAD SIGNS

The classification and numbering of "A" and "B" roads are indicated at road junctions in the following manner—"A" roads being shown in *black letters* and figures upon a *white ground* at the end of the sign-post arm, while "B" roads are shown in *white letters* upon a *black ground*, thus :—

| A744 | LONDON 35¾ | LUTON 4¼ | B479 |
|---|---|---|---|

The novelty and the unfamiliarity of the Ministry of Transport's road classification system also earned it prominent exposure in many road atlases of the 1920s. We can be pretty certain the road numbers shown in the illustration are a figment of pure imagination, however!

Clearly, there were some disadvantages to Michelin's proposals. But the letter and its enclosures were, according to the acknowledgement sent by Henry P. Maybury, 'being examined with much interest'. Sir Julian Orde of the Royal Automobile Club was also consulted, before the Ministry eventually decided upon the scheme that was inaugurated in 1922. But the extent to which André Michelin or Sir Julian Orde might have influenced the outcome here in the British Isles remains to be seen.

## The first numbers are allocated

The scheme that was adopted is fairly well understood. Great Britain was divided into nine sectors, six of which radiated in a clockwise order from London, and the remaining three, which radiated from Edinburgh. Thus:

A1 – London to Edinburgh

A2 – London to Dover

A3 – London to Portsmouth (the opening of the Guildford Bypass in the early 1930s caused a decision to be made to leave the sector boundary as the old road, rather than transfer it to the new route, which would thus cause a local renumbering of roads that would then commence in a different sector)

A4 –London to Bath

A5 – London to Holyhead

A6 – London to Carlisle (then actually started from the A1 at Barnet)

A7 – Edinburgh to Carlisle

A8 – Edinburgh to Gourock

A9 – Edinburgh to Inverness

Originally sector 1 included all the roads situated between roads A1 and A2, and so on for the remaining nine sectors. However, a change was very soon made to make the boundary between sectors 1 and 2 the River Thames, as opposed to the A2 road (although a few roads beginning with the number 1 do correctly continue south of the River!).

All roads took their initial number from the sector in which they started, but main routes kept their number even after crossing over the boundary into the next sector. The commencement of any one road was determined by the end that would be reached first by the hands of a clock radiating from London. Thus the A27, for example, commenced at Brighton, and not at its junction with the A36. In sector 1 for example, all the A roads were numbered from A1–A19 and then A100 onwards if the number of main routes warranted using the higher numbers. When the B roads came up for numbering later in the scheme, these were allocated three or four digit numbers (it is said that route numbers were first introduced around 1919 when some Class I roads were allocated 'A' numbers and some Class II roads 'B' numbers).

The first classification was a provisional one, and local authorities could submit their own changes or amendments if they wished. But in February 1923 the Ministry of Transport could write to all the County and Metropolitan Boroughs confirming the final scheme of classification for all Class I and II roads. This was to be used from 1 April 1923 for all purposes connected with the Ministry, including the submission of estimates and returns of expenditure relative to maintenance and improvement grants. The local authorities were sent detailed classification schedules for checking and amendment of the mileages, which had been altered in some instances by the Ministry. The letter also acknowledged that official maps, at the scale of ½ inch to 1 mile showing the Class 1 and Class 2 roads, and their numbers, were in the course of preparation by the Ordnance Survey and that it was hoped that these would be on sale by April 1923.

Regular revision of road numbers justified the sale – and purchase – of new road maps both in the mid-1920s and today.

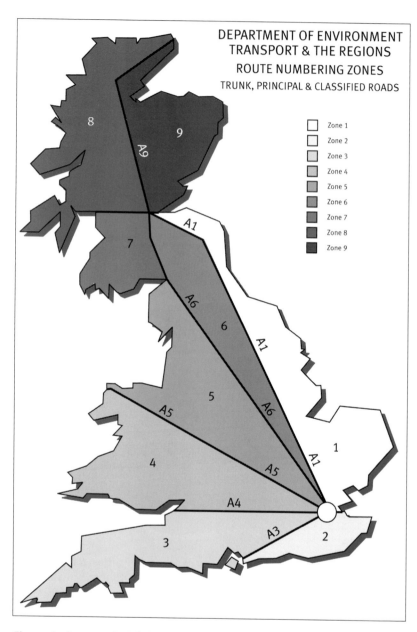

The numbering zones for Britain's A and B roads (but not the motorways) are shown in this official map.

The Ministry requested that local authorities added the route numbers to existing direction posts and signs, noting that the costs incurred in this exercise were chargeable to the expenditure ranking for grant under the classification scheme. Comprehensive instructions appeared in 1925 as part of a Ministry of Transport memorandum entitled 'Recommendations for the Standardisation of Road Direction Posts and Warning Signs'. This specified that first class roads should be signed with a black letter A and figures on a white ground and second class roads with a white letter B and figures on a black ground.

Direction signs have included road numbers for many decades now, with only minor changes in presentation.

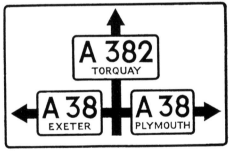

## Numbers appear on road maps

Various maps entitled 'Ministry of Transport Road Map' were published at the scale of ½ inch to 1 mile. For England and Wales, these were based on the Half-inch Map of England and Wales. This series comprised 40 sheets, with sheet number 4 covering the Isle of Man. Sheets 1–3 and 5–40 were thus produced showing the road classification for the year 1922–3. Since the Ministry of Transport had no jurisdiction in the Isle of Man, there was no need to produce sheet 4 as an MoT map, as the island was not included in the scheme (in any case, the Isle of Man's own road numbering system was not devised until nearly 30 years later).

Class I roads had their numbers only shown in red and Class II roads had their numbers only shown in green (in purple by 1936–7). Letters were not shown on the map and a note indicated that Class I numbers should be prefixed with the letter 'A' and Class II numbers with the letter 'B'.

At this scale, no detail was provided on the maps for the central London area. Six sheets at the scale of 2 inches to the mile were therefore produced to cover central London. These also showed the classification for the year 1922–23, but it should be noted that there were, at that time, no classified roads in the City of London (the City did not officially join the system until 1 April 1928). No later editions of the six 2-inches-to-the-mile London sheets have been noted.

For Scotland, the MoT road maps were based on the Half-inch Map of Scotland. This series comprised 34 sheets, seven of which covered the

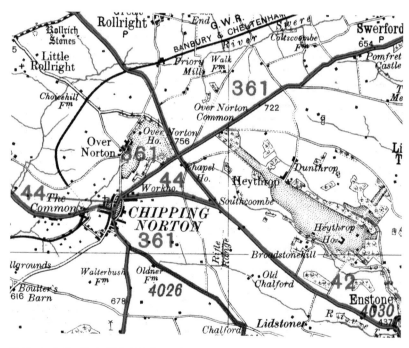

Confusingly the first official Ministry of Transport road maps did not show letters, only numbers. On the actual roads direction signs showed letters and numbers, however. This extract illustrates the kind of changes that have occurred in the last 80 years: the A361 and B4026 remain unaltered but the A42 was subsequently renumbered A34. The section north of Southcoombe is now the A3400, whilst the southern section here has become part of the A44.

New road numbers called for new guide posts and many counties adopted this pattern of sign. Many detail differences can still be seen around the country, with highway authorities favouring the products of a number of different foundries. This design was common in Oxfordshire.

various island groups off the north-east and western coasts. All the sheets for Scotland were thus produced showing the road classification for the year 1922–3, just as for England and Wales. The Ordnance Survey produced two further maps in 1932 at the scale of 10 miles to one inch. These two sheets were titled *ROAD MAP OF GREAT BRITAIN showing the NUMBERS and CLASSIFICATION of the MINISTRY OF TRANSPORT.* Later on, the road numbers were added to the ordinary Ordnance Survey maps, along with their 'A' or 'B' prefixes. This obviated the need for separate maps to show the classification and numbering system.

The Ordnance Survey did not have a monopoly of maps showing the new numbers and other publishers soon followed suit. The *Daily Mail* newspaper also issued maps that were among the first commercial publications to include the new road numbers.

In 1923 an official list was published by H.M.S.O. showing route numbers and details of the main towns through which they passed. This list also included numbers allocated to several 'proposed new roads' and several new roads 'in course of construction'. This list was included in a book

Where highway authorities did not erect signs with the new numbers the Royal Automobile Club stepped in with signs made in its own factory at Victoria, London. This 1936 photograph shows a selection of signs for mainly South Coast destinations plus Southend on the B842 (which is on the southern coast of Kintyre in Scotland).

entitled *List of Class I and II Roads and Numbers – Record of Amendments 1923–1926.* A second list was published in 1926 that incorporated all the amendments noted in this book. This second list was also included in a new book entitled *List of Class I and II Roads and Numbers – Record of Amendments 1927–1930.* This differed slightly from the first book, by including a map reference and a regional reference (M = Midlands, N = Northern, L = London, for example). Only the first list appears to have gone on general sale to the public, although official correspondence suggests that copies of the later lists were made available to Highway Authorities in some instances.

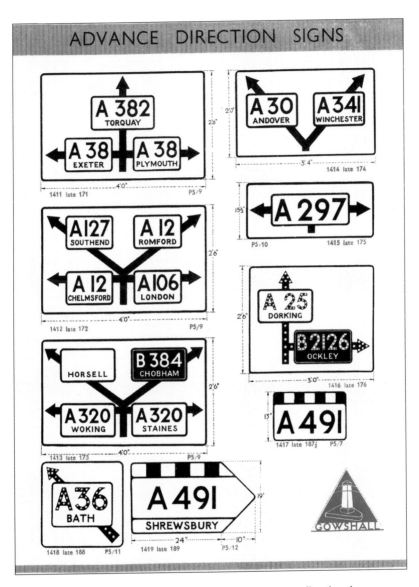

Until new 'Continental' signage appeared in the late 1960s most direction signs conformed to a style devised three decades previously. The chequered stripe indicated a road leading to the numbered destination shown and signs for B roads were distinguished by white lettering on black. Some signs used glass reflectors in the lettering to make their legends more visible in the dark.

# ANALYSIS OF A-ROADS

| Number ranges: | Description: | No: | Notes: |
|---|---|---|---|
| A1 | London (Goswell Road) – Edinburgh | 1 | The old 'Great North Road' |
| A10–19 | 10–13 radiate from London and 14–19 are provincial roads | 10 | |
| A100–199 | 100–103 are London local roads, 104–118 are of London area origin, the rest are provincial | 100 | |
| A1000–1064 | 1000–1011 are of London area origin, the rest are provincial | 65 | 11 are described using the work 'Link' |
| A1200–1209 | London local roads | 10 | All relatively short links |
| | **Total of A-numbers used in sector 1** | **186** | |
| A2 | London (Great Dover Street) – Folkestone | 1 | The Old 'Dover Road' |
| A20–29 | 20–24 are of London area origin, the rest are provincial | 10 | |
| A200–288 | 200–219 are of London area origin, the rest are provincial | 89 | |
| A2000–2011 | Provincial local roads | 12 | 9 are described using the word 'link' |
| A2200–2217 | London local roads | 18 | All relatively short links |
| | **Total of A-numbers used in sector 2** | **130** | |
| A3 | London (London Bridge) – Portsmouth | 1 | The old 'Portsmouth Road'. |
| A30–39 | All provincial roads, although the A30 commences in the London area by a junction with the A4 near Cranford) | 10 | |
| A300–399 | 300–304 are London local roads and 305–399 are provincial roads | 100 | |
| A3000–3048 | All provincial roads (many are short links) | 49 | 8 are described using the word 'link'; 3020–3023 are on the Isle of Wight |
| A3200–3218 | London local roads | 19 | All relatively short links |
| | **Total of A-numbers used in sector 3** | **179** | |
| A4 | London (Strand) – Bath | 1 | The old 'Bath Road' |
| A40–49 | All provincial roads, although the A40 starts at London (High Holborn) | 10 | |
| A400–499 | 400–407 are of London area origin, the rest are provincial | 100 | |
| A4000–4087 | 4000–4007 are of London area origin, the rest are provincial | 88 | 17 are described using the word 'link' |
| A4200–4207 | London local roads | 8 | Mostly relatively short links |
| | **Total of A-numbers used in sector 4** | **207** | |

| A5 | London (Edgware Road) – Holyhead | 1 | The old London-Holyhead Road |
|---|---|---|---|
| A50–59 | All provincial roads | 10 | |
| A500–597 | 500–504 are of London area origin, the rest are provincial | 98 | |
| A5000–5076 | 5000 runs from Hendon to Finchley in London, the rest are provincial | 77 | 23 are described using the word 'link' |
| A5200–5203 | London local roads | 4 | All relatively short links |
| | **Total of A-numbers used in sector 5** | **190** | |
| A6 | Chipping Barnet – Carlisle | 1 | |
| A60–A69 | All provincial roads | 10 | |
| A600–699 | All provincial roads | 100 | |
| A6000–6096 | All provincial roads | 97 | 42 are described using the word 'link' |
| | **Total of A-numbers used in sector 6** | **208** | |
| A7 | Carlisle – Edinburgh | 1 | |
| A70–78 | All provincial roads | 9 | |
| A700–742 | All provincial roads | 43 | 1 is described using the word 'link' |
| | **Total of A-numbers used in sector 7** | **53** | |
| A8 | Edinburgh – Gourock | 1 | |
| A80–88 | All provincial roads | 9 | |
| A800–859 | All provincial roads | 60 | 4 are described using the word 'link'; 841–3 are on the Island of Arran; 844/845 are on the Island of Bute; 846/847 are on Islay; 848/849 are on the Island of Mull; 850–856 are on the Isle of Skye; 857–859 are on the Isle of Lewis |
| | **Total of A-numbers used in sector 8** | **70** | |
| A9 | Edinburgh – Inverness | 1 | |
| A90–98 | All provincial roads | 9 | |
| A900–954 | All provincial roads | 55 | 3 are described using the word 'link' |
| A960–971 | All provincial roads | 12 | 1 is described using the word 'link'; 960–967 are on Mainland (Orkney Islands); 968–971 are on Mainland (Shetland Islands). |
| | **Total of A-numbers used in sector 9** | **77** | |
| | **TOTAL OF ALL A-NUMBERS USED** | **1300** | |

# ANALYSIS OF B-ROADS

| Number ranges: | Description: | No: | Notes: |
|---|---|---|---|
| B100–125 | All London local roads | 26 | |
| B150–B189 | 150–167 are London local roads and 168–189 are provincial roads, but all of which are relatively close to London | 40 | 6 are described using the word 'link' |
| B1000–1350 | All provincial roads | 351 | 35 are described using the word 'link' |
| | **Total of B-numbers used in sector 1** | **417** | |
| B200–235 | All London local roads | 36 | |
| B250–258 | All relatively close to London | 9 | 1 is described using the word 'link' |
| B260–290 | All relatively close to London | 31 | 3 are described using the word 'link' |
| B2000–2155 | All provincial roads (The (259) also appears in this section of the listing after the B2107 but the number is shown in brackets. This is assumed to be a typographical error for the A259, which follows a similar course.) | 156 | 28 are described using the word 'link' |
| | **Total of B-numbers used in sector 2** | **232** | |
| B300–318 | All London local roads | 19 | |
| B350–B389 | All relatively close to London | 40 | 4 are described using the word 'link' |
| B3000–3332 | All provincial roads | 333 | 20 are described using the word 'link'; 3320–3332 are on the Isle of Wight |
| | **Total of B-numbers used in sector 3** | **392** | |
| B400–414 | All London local roads | 15 | |
| B450–489 | All relatively close to London | 40 | 3 are described using the word 'link' |
| B4000–4424 | All provincial roads | 425 | 25 are described using the word 'link' |
| | **Total of B-numbers used in sector 4** | **480** | |
| B500–519 | All London local roads | 20 | |
| B550–589 | 550–554 are London local roads, the rest are provincial | 40 | 7 are described using the word 'link' |
| B5000–5307 | All provincial roads | 308 | 38 are described using the word 'link' |
| | **Total of B-numbers used in sector 5** | **368** | |

| Number ranges: | Description: | No: | Notes: |
|---|---|---|---|
| B650–689 | All provincial roads | 40 | 7 are described using the word 'link'; numbers 600–649 are not used |
| B6000–6374 | All provincial roads | 375 | 32 are described using the word 'link' |
| | **Total of B-numbers used in sector 6** | **415** | |
| B700–791 | All provincial roads | 92 | 2 are described using the word 'link' |
| | **Total of B-numbers used in sector 7** | **92** | |
| B800–898 | All provincial roads | 99 | 1 is described using the word 'link'; 888–890 are on the island of South Uist; 891–894 are on the island of North Uist; 895–898 are on the Isle of Lewis. |
| | **Total of B-numbers used in sector 8** | **99** | |
| B900–999 | All provincial roads | 100 | 10 are described using the word 'link' |
| B9000–9034 | All provincial roads | 35 | 3 are described using the word 'link' |
| B9040–9088 | All provincial roads | 49 | 3 are described using the word 'link'; 9040–9070 are on the Orkney Islands; 9071–9088 are on the Shetland Islands. |
| | **Total of B-numbers used in sector 9** | **184** | |
| | **TOTAL OF ALL B-NUMBERS USED** | **2679** | |

A study of this analysis does show that there is some science to the numbering system. Some of the number blocks are allocated to the London area only, for example, and there are also some gaps left in the numbers for future expansion. There are no 4-digit A-road numbers in zones 7, 8 or 9. There are no 4-digit B-roads in zones 7 or 8. The island groups around Scotland all have their own number blocks (it is interesting to note that numbers B600–649 are not used, which might be a reflection of the fact that zone 6 is very small nearest to London; the A5 and A6 also meet for a while at St Albans).

The numbering system was, in its early days, subjected to an annual revision. In one area alone, some 17.5 per cent of the numbers had been done away with in the first few years. One of the reasons for this seems to be that there was a tendency to allocate a new number to any stretch of road between roads whose number began with one or two digits. Clearly, there were advantages to be gained by amalgamating some of the previ-

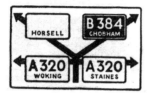

Fig. 41 (contd.).—As you approach a multiple crossing, these new signposts are often to be seen. Note that the road numbers have predominance. (The illustration does not actually show the Staines-Woking crossing.)

Direction signs with road numbers were evidently still a novelty in 1934, when this illustration was published.

ously separately numbered roads, which together still formed a through route. There were also instances where very short stretches of Class I roads were given their own separate identification usually with four digit numbers. This may have been a deliberate policy. Once again, many of these numbers disappeared as the scheme settled down after the first few years. As a later example of amalgamating two roads that previously had separate numbers, the present A325 south of Farnham was originally numbered the A326. This was also complicated by the fact that the A325 north of Farnham did not join the A326 south of Farnham.

The interests of the motorist can thus be seen at this stage to have over-ridden the initial importance of the classification system itself. However, later on, it became increasingly difficult to make major changes, as the cost of altering signs on routes that already ran for hundreds of miles would have been enormous. Minor changes were much easier to make if these were justified. Comparing, for example, the 1922–1923 and 1927–1928 issues of sheet 33 alone, the following changes may be noted:

| 1922–1923 sheet 33 | 1927–1928 sheet 33 |
| --- | --- |
| A287 from the A32 to the A30 | Has become the A3052 |
| None | New B3348 through Finchampstead |
| None | New B3349 from A327 to A329 |
| B3029 | Superseded by extension of A321 |
| None | New B4446 from A4 to B478 |
| B3048 | Extended north of A30 to Hurstbourne Tarrant |
| B3042 | Has become A3057 |
| B3085 | Has become A3052 |

*The Autocar* of 16 April 1921 had observed that some 36,000 miles of roads were included in Classes 1 and 2 for grant aid, but that 141,107 miles of third class roads were not included. It also observed that the £8,500,000 anticipated to be the first year's revenue for grants from the Road Fund, was better spent on just the Class 1 and Class 2 roads, on which a significant improvement could now be made, rather than spread thinly over the whole network.

Today the system remains much as it was introduced 80-odd years ago but some changes to the numbering system followed the opening of arterial roads in the 1930s and many more recent bypasses (sometimes originally referred to as bye-passes).

## County or 'C' roads

An addition to the classification scheme was the 'county roads' introduced by the Local Government Act, 1929. This required, among other things, that County Councils should become the highway authority for all 'main' roads. All other roads for which the county was the highway authority were to be called 'county roads'.

In Norfolk for example, all the 'county roads' were numbered as one system throughout the county, when this legislation was introduced. A map, dating from that time, and showing the whole 'C' road system is still retained by the Norfolk County Council's Planning & Transportation Department. Norfolk went even further than this by showing the 'C' road numbers on many village signs (in 1989, the village sign for Burnham Market, Norfolk, still showed the road number of C156 above the name).

But Norfolk was unusual. Although some other counties had adopted a system for identifying 'county roads' before the Second World War, many counties took no such action and did not introduce 'C' road numbers until Class III roads were officially instituted in 1946.

In Surrey, the county introduced a system of numbering the smaller roads only in 1938. In a schedule dated 18 May 1938, Bagshot Rural Division included the C1–C29 (inclusive), and for example, the D5, D7, D2/30, D1/322 and E14. The letters C, D and E represented the road width, and the designations that included two numbers appear to indicate that the road was a cul-de-sac off the road whose number was indicated last in the designation. Other designation styles were also used for some smaller connecting roads and some very small cul-de-sacs. (In the same schedules: Dorking and Horley Division included C road numbers in the range C132–C186; Godstone Rural Division included C road numbers in the range C182–C243; Guildford Rural Division included C road numbers in the range C30–C140; Hambledon Rural Division included C road numbers in the range C57–C145.)

These numbering systems were necessarily either county-wide or local, based on the local administrative area for highways. A single through road could therefore have its number changed at an administrative boundary, and certainly at the county boundary.

365 366 367

Road signs for C roads evidently had a coloured background (possibly yellow), as this illustration from a Gowshall trade catalogue of 1931 indicates. The actual shade used is unclear, however, as the book was not printed in full colour.

## Trunk roads

For the most important through roads, the situation whereby each local authority looked after different stretches of the same road didn't really work in practice. This, coupled with the fact that each county had its own surveyor with individual ideas about where improvements should take place, meant that there would always be a lack of countrywide co-ordination and co-operation. The only answer was for the State to take over control of the most important roads.

Thus on 18 December 1936 the Trunk Roads Act 1936 came into force. This piece of legislation created a network of 'principal roads in Great Britain constituting the national system of routes for through traffic which by virtue of the Act become trunk roads'. These, and any future road that became a trunk road, were overseen by the Ministry of Transport, which became the highway authority for these roads with effect from 1 April 1937. The Act listed all 30 of the routes that were included in the network, totalling in all some 4,459 miles. The trunk roads in Scotland were only included from 16 May 1937. The Act did not apply to Northern Ireland. The Minister would now be able to take an overview and co-ordinate the planning of improvements throughout the whole length of one of these main routes. He would use the county councils as his agents for doing the actual improvement works though.

It is often not appreciated that the routes did not always each comprise one numbered 'A' road. Although in the case of the London–Norwich, London–Great Yarmouth, London–Brighton, London–Portsmouth, London–Bristol, Chester–Bangor, Edinburgh–Carlisle, Edinburgh–Glasgow and Tyndrum–Oban trunk roads they did, the others comprised stretches of two or more separately numbered roads. However, in this first schedule of trunk roads, all the roads affected were 'A' roads.

The Trunk Roads Act 1936 (Substitution of New Routes) Order 1937 [Statutory Rules and Orders (1937), No. 211], made 28 specific variations to these new trunk roads, where a by-pass or diversion had been under construction or planned at the time the 1936 Act had been passed. A further 68 amendments were made in 1939 [Statutory Rules and Orders (1939), No. 235] and others have been made since then.

On 6 March 1946, a further 71 routes were added to the list by the Trunk Roads Act 1946, taking the total mileage to over 8,000. These additional roads became trunk roads with effect from 1 April 1946. The 1936 Act had excluded trunk roads from London and in the county boroughs, but this was now changed. The trunk roads now ran throughout from one end to another, regardless of the status of an area. The only exception was the City of London, which still contained no trunk roads.

Signs indicating C roads are extremely uncommon but do occur locally, such as this example on Kingston Park Road, Newcastle-upon-Tyne.

Some of these later routes now traversed 'B' roads and 'Unclassified' roads, as well as 'A' roads. The Act also gave the Minister powers to construct a bridge over, or tunnel under, navigable waters, thus avoiding the necessity of further special legislation in every separate case. This Act also did not apply in Northern Ireland. Trunk roads have usually been shown on later Ordnance Survey maps with the letter 'T' in brackets,

Aspirations of the 1930s for uncongested new trunk and arterial roads are illustrated well in this catalogue cover graphic.

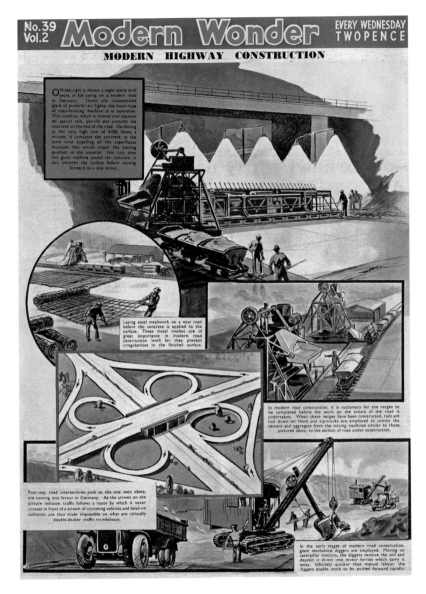

The building of new roads occupied many minds in the inter-war years, with considerable attention paid to new construction methods. The Cement & Concrete Association campaigned strongly for new motorways and even this boys' comic of 1938 caught the enthusiasm. In the event economic conditions meant that no motorways and only a few sections of dual carriageway A-roads were built in Britain before war broke out.

Cloverleaf junctions and cross-country motorways may have been a reality in pre-war Germany but were destined to remain a dream for roadbuilders in Britain. New road construction was directed at more urgent projects such as the pioneering Silvertown Way (A1020) in London. It was opened in September 1934 and is seen almost complete in the background in this view of Barking Road in Canning Town. It was Britain's first elevated urban highway, a mile long, 108 feet wide and 25 feet above the surrounding ground. The road's dual purpose was to relieve unemployment and the acute congestion at the entry to the docks of east London. Most of the construction remains.

after the road number. However, this designation is not applied to the road signs themselves (the National series of road maps produced by National fuel products company in the 1970s went as far as showing trunk roads as a different designation from other primary routes).

Both sets of trunk roads and all the various amendments were taken into the Highways Act 1959, Section 7, which consolidated the two previous Acts. With effect from 1 April 1956, the powers in respect of Scotland had been transferred to the Secretary of State for Scotland, who now became the highway authority. With effect from 1 April 1965, the powers in respect of Wales and Monmouth were transferred to the Secretary of State for Wales, who now became the highway authority.

In the last 55 years, there have been many changes to the trunk road network. Some roads, or stretches of road, have been de-trunked, or upgraded. Some of these changes have also occasioned changes to their road numbers. Today, Highway Authorities maintain a set of maps (produced by a special department of the Ordnance Survey, but not apparently available to the general public) showing the full classification scheme, including the 'C' and 'D' roads.

## Class III roads

A new road classification, known as Class III roads, was officially instituted by the Ministry of Transport with effect from 1 April 1946. This was an administrative action, not reflected in new road numbering, and was done purely to increase the mileage of roads on which improvement and maintenance were eligible for grant. Class III roads were those considered of more than local traffic importance.

The Ministry of Transport's justification to the Treasury for the institution of a Class III road network was based primarily on the importance of these roads to agriculture. But although most of these roads would be rural roads, some urban roads had to be included, as they would otherwise be ineligible for grant aid of any kind.

When the Class III designation for roads was introduced, some counties already had road numbers prefixed with the letter 'C', as noted earlier. However, the Ministry decided that, 'there be no national system of C.

Roads for the present'. It was noted, however, that some numbering system would be necessary for administrative purposes, 'but there was no reason why any existing numbers used by a highway authority should not continue to be used'. But of course, those counties that already used a numbering system for 'county roads' would find that not all 'county roads' could be classified as Class III roads. To simply do this would not conform with the Ministry's requirements. Those counties that had not previously used the 'C' road designation could now introduce some form of numbering for Class III roads. In one instance, this was just simply a number without any letter prefix. Some counties have also since used further designations for more minor roads (not in Class I, II or III) using prefixes such as 'D', 'U' or 'X' but these are not official designations.

## A Roman road sign in Surrey?

In the county of Surrey, the previous numbering system used for unclassified roads was now revised to include a new numbering sequence for Class III roads. These were shown on a map dated 1947. In the rural districts, roads CX1–CX92 were shown allocated roughly west-east across the county. Additional higher numbers were allocated in Urban Districts and Boroughs, up to about CX228. The map shows the CX11 and CX12 including Chobham Road and Limecroft Road, Knaphill. Forty years ago travellers might have been puzzled by the four finger-boards (since removed) on a signpost at a crossroads in the village of Knaphill, near Woking in Surrey. These were black lettering on a white background, two of which showed CXI and two of which showed CXII alongside respective destination place names.

A recent telephone call to the County Highways Authority revealed that these roads were now actually the C11 and the C12 (Chobham Road and Limecroft Road/High Street respectively). But it is not known when the signs date from. But as the X of CX is missing, it must be after that designation was changed. Is this the only instance of 'C' road numbers appearing on direction posts in Roman numerals?

## Other strange survivals

Official notices of temporary minor road closures, and the necessary diversionary routes, often appear in local papers. The roads will sometimes be referred to by their relevant 'A', 'B', 'C' or 'D' numbers. Locally, Surrey County Council does show the 'C' and 'D' road numbers, but Hampshire County Council has used road names alone in these instances. These 'C' and 'D' numbers rarely appear on direction signs, however, though there have been several instances of them appearing in the past. The C16A, Delves Lane, in County Durham acquired two signs that showed the road number on them in error. Although the mistake was spotted, the cost in changing them immediately was thought not to be justified. However, the authorities in County Durham have more recently observed that as the signs are 'now nearing the end of their useful life it is likely they will be replaced as part of routing maintenance in the near future'.

Direction signs that indicate 'C' roads can be found all over the British Isles and Chris Marshall's database of British Roads on the Internet has a whole section devoted to what he calls 'The Great C Road Hunt' with lists and photos at http://www.cbrd.co.uk/c-roads. Similarly, the D1117 in Frensham, Surrey, also had a small signpost that showed just the number in white on a blue background. This may be a unique instance of a 'D' road number appearing on a signpost.

Occasionally, C-road numbers do appear on Ordnance Survey Maps, or maps that use OS maps as a base. For example, Alton Library have a Hampshire County Council Planning Department plan, ref: 22/4942 (scale 1:2500), dated September 1966, which is based on an OS map. This is titled 'Medstead Village Plan' and shows three C-roads: the C26 to Alresford and Alton; the C36 to Four Marks and Bentworth; the C138 to Wield and Four Marks. Other 1:1250 OS maps occasionally also show C-road numbers, but these are usually former Highway Department maps that have been passed to local libraries for their use. New C-roads are still being created, as in these recent examples:

Bentley Bypass (A31) – old A31 route downgraded to become a newly numbered road, the C70.

Runfold Diversion (A31) east of Farnham – old A31 downgraded, becoming an extension of the local road C119.

It is understood that 'C' and 'D' road numbers are still used for administrative purposes, but in Hampshire, for example, most new roads are given a 'U' number (the small cul-de-sac in which I live is the U227). 'U' stands for unclassified. Once again, these numbers do not appear on signs, but do enable highway authorities to accurately refer to individual roads for administrative purposes.

## Further changes in classification

Although the zonal numbering system and the 'A' and 'B' prefixes have continued right up to the present day, the same is not true of the principles of classification. The way in which grants are now paid is also different to the original fixed percentages in respect of each of the Class I, II and III systems.

The Highways Act 1959 was largely a measure to consolidate previous enactments, although it did include some amendments. It affected only

England and Wales. Class I, II and III roads (but not trunk roads) were abolished under the Local Government Act 1966, Section 27. The purpose was to then reclassify non-trunk roads as either 'principal' or 'non-principal'. Improvement schemes on 'principal' roads were still eligible for specific grants (Highways Act 1959, Section 235), but those on 'non-principal' roads were not, unless they were the result of a 'principal' road scheme. In practice, all 'A' roads and most 'B' roads became principal, but there were no changes to their numbers due to the reclassification.

This system changed once again under the Local Government Act of 1974 (Sections 1 and 6). Rather than being given specific grants on individual 'principal' road schemes, a grant was awarded on the basis of an authority's transport policies and executive programme. Expenditure on non-principal roads is therefore in effect eligible under this system. From henceforth, the classification of a road was no longer strictly tied to grant eligibility.

# 4
# THE MOTORWAY ERA
## A new layer of complexity

The history of Britain's motorways is strewn with might-have-been and misconception. The might-have-beens have a long heritage, dating back at least to a 1906 proposal for a dual-carriageway London-Brighton Motorway for which parliamentary approval was sought but not received. Timely it certainly was, pre-dating by one year the Long Island Motor Parkway in the USA, generally considered to have been the first motorway constructed.

British interest in motorways reawakened in the 1920s, when detailed plans were published for the Northern and Western Motorway of 1923 and a revised London-Brighton Motorway in 1925. The Northern and Western could be likened to a combination of today's M40 and M6; it was to begin on Western Avenue at Uxbridge and run close to Aylesbury and Leamington Spa (with a spur to Coventry), then passing west of Birmingham, Wolverhampton, Stafford and Stoke, leading to a point on the south side of Manchester and a projected spur to Liverpool.

Jonathan Winkler, who has carried out detailed research into these early motorway plans, notes that in line with Italy's thinking for its first *autostrada*, all of these projects envisaged a single (undivided) carriageway (except at junctions) and it was not until 1933 that the Ministry of Transport indicated that all new roads expected to carry more than 400 vehicles per hour at peak times should be constructed as dual carriageways. A number of new roads were constructed in this fashion, notably the A24 Mickleham Bypass in Surrey, the A580 East Lancashire Road and a number of arterial roads in outer London, such as the Great West Road (A4), Western Avenue (A40) and the A127 to Southend. All of these were all-purpose roads, however, and were not built to a specification that we would recognise today as motorways.

Pressure to construct motorways resumed during the Second World War, a time when many protagonists published imaginative plans for better times to come. A 1946 book, *The Royal Road*, illustrated graphically the way motorways could blend with "the most beautiful countryside" and quoted Mr P.J. Noel-Baker, Minister of State, as being convinced that motorways would be built "within the next thirty years". Such confidence!

HAROLD PE

Although Britain's first motorway did not open until 1958, many detailed proposals were published before then, as this 1944 impression from 'New Roads for Britain' exemplifies. The artist has visualised "one of the rest house sites, where first-class refreshment and sleeping accommodation will be available on one side of the road, with fuel and vehicle service facilities on both sides. A motor subway connects the two."

## Britain's first motorway

So much for the might-have-beens. The misconception (a very widespread one) is that our first motorway was the M1. In fact the first was opened with great fanfare on 5th December 1958, just four hours before Britain's first motorway casualty occurred. It was of course the short Preston Bypass, built from the outset to motorway standards and later incorporated into the M6 motorway. The first section of the M1 opened in April 1960 and was then known as the London-Birmingham Motorway since it was a northern terminal as at Dunchurch, where an upgraded A45 continued the route to Birmingham. Later its target was refocused on Leeds and the M1 was renamed the London-Yorkshire Motorway. Inconsistency of naming characterised some other early motorways; the M2 was termed the Medway Towns Motor Road in early publications for instance.

Although the Preston Bypass assumed the road number A6 upon opening, the introduction of further motorways called for revision of the numbering system. These roads were built under the enabling legislation of the Special Roads Act of 1949, since consolidated by the Highways Acts of 1959 and 1980. A special Act was required, as users did not have the same total right of access to these roads as they did on other public highways. The motorways are prefixed with the letter M and often (but not always) numbered to correspond to the main routes that they parallel (this might have been to deliberately encourage longer distance drivers to use the M route rather than the roughly parallel A route). Some A roads have also been reconstructed in recent years to a standard similar to that of motorways and these sections of road usually have the letter M shown in brackets after the A road number, such as A1(M).

## Motorway numbering

From the outset, motorway numbering has followed different rules from other roads. Policy files in the National Archives indicate that at one stage it was intended that the main motorways would have only single digit numbers, with all spurs numbered starting with the same main motorway number. That is why the first spur off the M1 is M10. Three digit numbers were intended only for use within the main city ring motorways then proposed, such as London, Birmingham and Manchester.

This upbeat brochure issued by Shell-Mex and BP Ltd typifies the enthusiasm felt for motorway development in 1960. The London-Birmingham motorway (A) is shown on the map as started, whilst the others planned are (B) the Birmingham–Preston–Lancaster motorway, (C) the London–South Wales motorway, (D) the Birmingham–Bristol motorway, (E) the London–Yorkshire motorway, (F) the Ross Spur motorway and (G) the Medway Towns motorway.

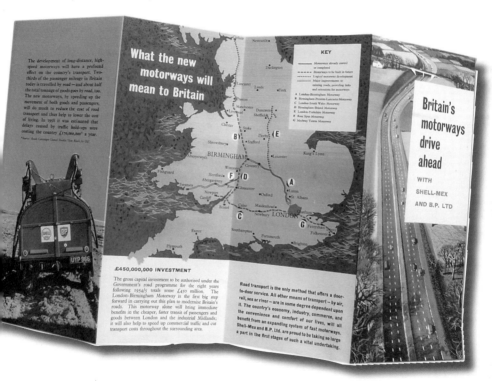

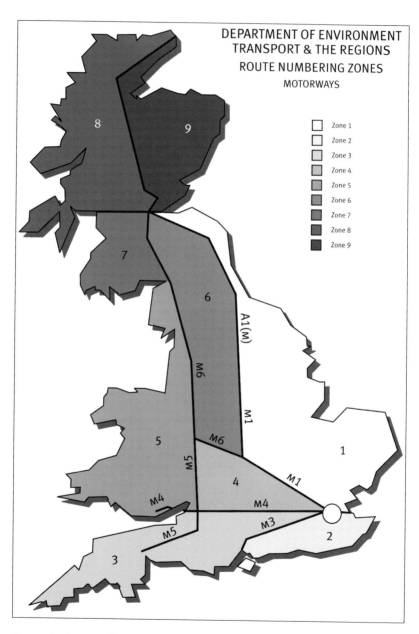

The numbering zones for motorways differ from those that apply to A and B roads (see page 26), as this official map indicates.

A current official map showing the route numbering zones for motorways shows how these zones differ from those used for Trunk, Principal and Classified Roads. The M1 and A1(M) form the boundary for zone 1; the M3 is the boundary between zones 2 and 3; the M4 between London and the Bristol Channel is the boundary between zones 3 and 4; Wales, west of the M5 becomes zone 5, which zone also extends northwards to include the area west of the M6. Zone 6 is therefore that area east of the M6 and west of the M1/A1(M). The three zones covering Scotland, zones 7, 8 and 9, remain the same for all types of road. The Department for Transport is the traffic regulation authority for all motorways in England and Wales, as well as the trunk roads.

## MOTORWAY NUMBERS THAT HAVE BEEN USED TO DATE:

| M1 | London to Wetherby |
|---|---|
| M2 | Rochester to Faversham |
| M3 | Sunbury to Southampton |
| M4 | London to South Wales |
| M5 | Birmingham to Exeter |
| M6 | Rugby to Carlisle (there is also a new duplicate toll road section designated 'M6 Toll') |
| M8 | Edinburgh to east of Coatbridge and west of Coatbridge to Bishopston |
| M9 | Edinburgh to Dunblane |
| M10 | Part of St Albans bypass |
| M11 | London to Cambridge |
| M12 | A proposed London to Colchester and Ipswich motorway. The number was applied to the South Woodford to Brentwood Bypass and appeared in some reports and other literature. |
| M14 | London 'motorway box' (proposed Ringway 1) |
| M15 | London inner ring motorway (proposed Ringway 2) |
| M16 | Number allocated to a Dartford–South Mimms–Yeading motorway (Ringway 3) that would have followed a route largely equivalent to the M25. |
| M18 | Connects M1 to M62 |
| M20 | Swanley to Folkestone |
| M23 | Hooley to Crawley |
| M25 | London Orbital Motorway from Dartford to Thurrock |
| M26 | Connects M25 to M20 |
| M27 | Cadnam to Portsmouth |
| M31 | Proposed South Orbital Link Motorway, connecting M3 to M4 |
| M32 | Spur from M4 to Bristol |
| M40 | Uxbridge to M42 south of Birmingham, originally also from Edgware Road flyover to Shepherds Bush in London. |

| | |
|---|---|
| M41 | Spur from A40(M) in west London (designation only used for a short time in the mid 1980s). Later on it became the A41(M) and later still the A41. Further north the Berkhamsted bypass was planned as another element of a different M41. |
| M42 | Bromsgrove to A42 near Measham |
| M45 | Dunchurch Spur (M1 to A45 near Rugby) |
| M48 | The older M4 Severn Crossing, but now joining the M4 at either end |
| M49 | Bristol to M4 (second Severn Crossing) |
| M50 | Ross-on-Wye to M5 |
| M53 | Wallasey to Chester |
| M54 | Telford to M6 |
| M55 | From M6 north of Preston to Blackpool |
| M56 | Cheadle to north of Chester |
| M57 | Liverpool outer ring road |
| M58 | Liverpool to M6 |
| M60 | Manchester South Orbital Motorway |
| M61 | M62 to M6 near Preston |
| M62 | Liverpool to A63 west of Hull |
| M63 | Manchester outer ring road (from M62/M602 to Stockport/M66) |
| M65 | M61 to Colne |
| M66 | M67–M63 |
| M67 | Denton to Hattersley |
| M69 | Coventry to Leicester |
| M73 | M74 to Mollinsburn |
| M74 | Rutherglen to Abington |
| M77 | Dumbreck Spur, Glasgow (A77 near Newton Mearns to Glasgow) |
| M80 | Hagas to M9 at Stirling |
| M85 | Perth eastern bypass, now part of the diverted M90 |
| M90 | Forth road bridge to Perth |
| M180 | M18 to Brigg |
| M181 | M180 to Scunthorpe |
| M271 | Southampton to south of Romsey |
| M275 | Spur from M27 to Portsmouth |
| M602 | M62/M63 to Salford |
| M606 | Bradford to M62 |
| M621 | Leeds to M62 |
| M876 | M80 near Bonnybridge to Kincardine Bridge via part of M9 |
| M898 | Spur from M8 to Erskine Bridge |

## Named junctions

There is no doubt an art to designating motorway junctions. Most countries number them sequentially, starting at 1 although the Americans allot each junction its figure in miles from the state border. With its gaps, this scheme avoids all the problems of allocating A and B suffixes to accommodate junctions built after a motorway first opened. It also enables travellers to calculate distances along the motorway by subtracting the entry junction number from their exit point.

When the M1 opened, the planners must have had second thoughts about the memorability of numbers alone and gave the junctions names as well. Many of these names had rather an attractive ring to them, such as Berrygrove (J5), Waterdale (J6), Breakspears (J8), Friar's Wash (J9) and Pepperstock (J10). These colourful names have fallen into disuse but they set in motion a trend under which many junctions and roundabouts along main roads are now graced with names such as Tweentown Roundabout (Cheddar), Bottledump Roundabout (Milton Keynes), Boot and Shoe (Micklefield) and Speculation Inn junction (Pembrokeshire). Unofficial names include two Magic Roundabouts in Swindon and Hemel Hempstead, each so called because of the unusual road layouts the motorist encounters there.

## Orbital origins

Today's London Orbital Motorway, the M25, is the tangible result of many plans to build ring roads around London. A number of these plans date back to before the Second World War, with the first plans conceived in 1911. The North and South Circular Roads (A406 and A205 respectively) were early attempts to relieve congestion in central London but the spread of London has long since overrun these 'avoiding' routes.

One of the first of these was the so-called North Orbital Road, of which several sections were built along a route from Denham (Bucks) to Hatfield (Herts.), skirting Watford and St Albans. A wide alignment was allowed to enable the new road to be converted into dual carriageways later but this did not happen along the whole route, which itself was never completed entirely. These breaks mean that the sections, all named North Orbital Road but numbered variously A412, A405 and A414, cannot be followed as a through route.

A comprehensive reappraisal was carried out in Professor Abercrombie's 1944 *Greater London Plan*, which set out plans for a comprehensive hierarchy of American-influenced express routes, major arterial routes, sub-arterial routes and parkways (see glossary at the end of this book for explanations of these terms). Highly ambitious, few of these schemes reached fruition. Included in these was an array of ring roads around London (named with letters from A-E and not all planned as complete rings) at various radial distances from the central area.

Notable among them was Scheme D, an orbital 'express arterial road' or motorway that followed part of the route of today's M25 with some variations. For instance, it was projected to continue just south of Radlett and through Bushey (crossing what is now the M1 at the A411 underbridge) and on a south-westerly alignment through Pinnerwood golf-course, then turning south (skirting Park Wood to the east) to pick up the primary A4180 and A312 close to Yeading.

From the 1930s onwards, sections of a grandly named North Orbital Road were constructed in piecemeal fashion in Hertfordshire and Buckinghamshire. Effectively a forerunner of the M25 motorway, these ambitious plans for a ring road around London were never fully realised, leaving many gaps in what was to have been a continuous route. Seen in February 1935, a three-wheeled car passes a sign where a section of the London North Orbital road was started immediately south of the county boundary near West Hyde on what is now Denham Way (A412). Unsurprisingly, no trace of this road layout remains today.

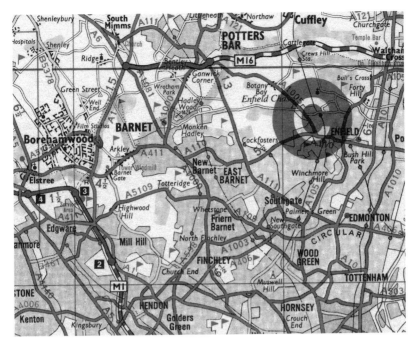

This is one of the rather few maps on which the short-lived M16 motorway number actually appeared. Also visible are the projected link between junction 3 of the M1 and the A1 together with the temporary London terminal of the M1 at Mill Hill (old junction 2).

## Ringways revealed

In the 1960s the number of rings planned in and around London was reduced to three, all to be of motorway construction and known as Ringways 1, 2 and 3. The innermost ring, Ringway 1 alias the 'Motorway Box', was the most controversial and, although intended to run above rooftops on elevated sections, would nevertheless have involved much demolition of property. In addition, the arterial trunk motorways entering London would have been extended to reach Ringway 1 and thus disruption together with the potential noise and pollution all ensured it was never brought to fruition.

Ringway 1 was conceived as the composite of four sections known as the North, East, South and West Cross routes. Only two fragments of the scheme were built: an interchange at Hackney Wick (where the North Cross route was to join the East Cross) and a short section of the West Cross route rear Shepherds Bush. The latter, originally designated the M14 and then M41 (both temporary numbers, see over), runs from

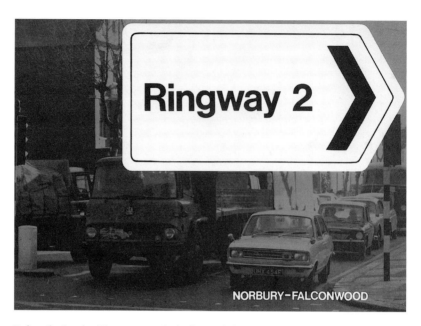

NORBURY–FALCONWOOD

Before the London Ringways reached advanced planning stage the Greater London Council went out to consultation, issuing detailed illustrated booklets such as the 1969 example above. The booklet included the map shown below.

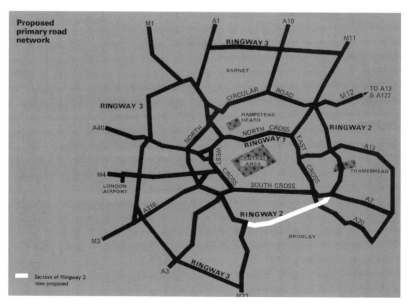

Shepherds Bush in the south to a half-finished interchange with the Westway. The East Cross route was intended to incorporate the existing Blackwall Tunnel and approach roads, which were designated A102(M) for a time, later renumbered the A12.

The intermediate motorway (Ringway 2, equivalent to Abercrombie's Scheme C) was to be known as the M15, incorporating an upgraded North Circular Road (A406). Politically controversial, it was not constructed.

## Orbital oddities

Ringway 3, the outermost of the proposals, was built, however, and is known today as the M25. This was not the original plan, which was to allocate separate numbers for the sections north and south of the Thames, M16 and M25 respectively. The first section to be built took the route of part of Abercrombie's Scheme D running eastwards from the A1 north of London. This road, from Bignell's Corner (South Mimms) to Ganwick Corner (Potters Bar) was christened the M16. Construction on the southeast side of London followed elements of Abercrombie's Scheme E and was designated the M25 and since this new M25 paralleled the A25 roughly for much of its route from the start point at the M26/M20 junction, there was some logic to the number it was given. This notion of designating two separate northern (M16) and southern (M25) motorways around London was abandoned in 1975 when it was announced that they would be amalgamated into one single ring, the London Orbital Motorway (M25). The M16 designation was now dropped, although not before it had made an appearance on several maps.

Because the M25 was constructed piecemeal, opening it in the form of isolated sections of motorway could have led to frustration and confusion and, instead, these sections were available to all traffic when opened. What was planned originally as the M16 east of the A1 was christened A1178 on opening in September 1975, later renumbered the A1005 before becoming the M25. Other parts of the future M25 were given provisional 'A' road numbers until the motorway was completed as a single entity too. An example is the section of the M25 between junctions 17 and 19a opened as the A405 (at this time the route of the M25 south of J17 was not yet decided).

## A record holder

The M25 number designation was eventually applied to the whole of the orbital motorway thus created (although technically the motorway does not form a true ring around London, as the Dartford Crossing and approaches are not of motorway status and have the designation A282). Bearing in mind the rules for determining the start of a road – working

Plans to build the M16 motorway through Epping Forest upset the villagers of Upshire. On 13th March 1974 they presented the Environment minister with this oversize 'potted plant'.

clockwise from London – there is some logic to the designation M25 being applied to the whole of the horseshoe shaped route, which really starts on the south side of the Thames and travels clockwise to the north side of the Thames. It holds a number of records: the longest city bypass in the world and sporadically the world's biggest car park (when accidents halt the traffic). The section skirting Heathrow Airport, opened in 2005, was Britain's first 12–lane highway and is also claimed as Europe's busiest motorway.

Incidentally, there appears to be some confusion over the original numbering of the three London Ringway schemes, with a suggestion that the Ringways 1, 2 and 3 were going to be numbered M41, M42 and M43. Another statement alleges that M43 was allocated to Ringway 2 rather than Ringway 3. In all probability a variety of numbers was proposed but considered opinion has it they were to be numbered M14, M15 and M16 respectively. There is evidence in print that Ringway 3's northern side was to be the M16 and that the east side of Ringway 2 was to be the M15. The theory then goes that the M14 was flipped to read M41 (a temporary number) either by accident or because, while this section was isolated, it fell within the 4–zone.

## 'Useless' motorways?

Some commentators have criticised the need for building certain early spur motorways, such as the M10 and M45 or else have misinterpreted the reason for their construction, claiming their purpose was to filter off traffic to reduce congestion at the actual terminals. Hindsight is the only 20:20 vision and these interpretations illustrate the danger of applying current-day analysis to a 1960 situation.

The M1 was opened as the London-Birmingham Motorway, conceived towards the end of the 1950s, a decade in whose first four years the country was experiencing rationing, severe austerity and a road and rail transport network that had seen no investment since the 1930s (which itself was for most of the time a period of miserable recession tempered only by some road construction as unemployment relief, e.g. the Thanet Way, and minor tinkering, e.g. the Kingston Bypass). There was simply no money for grandiose motorway schemes, so those plans that did look like they could be financed had to be designed for 'best value', integrated with the existing trunk road system. Whilst the Ministry of Transport did have plans for the M1 to become a London-Yorkshire motorway to relieve the A1, they could not afford this initially. Instead, the planners used what little budget they had to achieve maximum value.

It is worth recalling here the state of Britain's trunk roads at this time. The A1 was a single two-lane road passing through the very middle of congested town centres such as Stevenage, Baldock and Stamford, with many railway level crossings that were closed 50 per cent of the time, as in Newark. The A5 was similar, choked at Dunstable, Stony Stratford and 101 other places. Worst of all, the heavy lorries were hampered by a 20mph (unbelievable today) speed restriction at the beginning of the decade and most were owned by British Road Services, a nationalised organisation that was not endowed with generous funds for investing in new lorries. The net result was a crawling, under-funded road network with no immediate prospect of major improvement.

In preparation for the time when the M1 would run as far as Yorkshire they built the M10, to provide a connection for traffic accustomed to the Great North Road exit from London. Meanwhile, the combination of M1 and M45 provided some relief for freight vehicles bound for Coventry and Birmingham, and after the Crick spur was opened, for vehicles going north on the A5. At the same time the existing A45 road was upgraded to dual carriageway between the end of the M45 and Coventry. In addition the A5 north of Crick was widened out to three lanes; most of the dualled sections came later. Summing up, the M1 as built with its M10 and M45 spurs was not ill-conceived but a masterly piece of 'make do and mend'.

# 5
# CAPITAL HIGHWAYS
## The streets of London: a special case

In many ways the complex nature of London's road system marks it out as worthy of special study, which is why the subject is given a chapter of its own.

Since Roman times London has been the focal point of Britain's road network and the convergence of so many main roads gave an enhanced status to many streets of inner London. Indeed, when 'principal' roads were introduced in 1966, almost all metropolitan roads and many non-metropolitan (Borough) roads were declared 'principal'.

When the original road numbering scheme was announced in 1923, and the various maps and the list of road numbers published, it became apparent that no classified roads penetrated the City of London boundary. The reason was that the Streets Committee of the City of London, although aware that the Ministry of Transport was planning to introduce road numbers, took the view 'that the Corporation should take no action in the matter'. This was against the repeated advice of the City Engineer, who pointed out that substantial funds could be claimed from the Ministry of Transport to defray paving work expenditure.

Only at the beginning of 1928 was there at last a move to classify the City's roads, with a definite scheme finally submitted in February 1928. Just 8.83 miles of Class I roads and 3.51 miles of Class II roads were added to the national classification scheme as a result of the City's inclusion! The details were as follows:

| Route number: | Description of Road: | Names of Roads or Streets: | Mileage: | Author's Notes: |
|---|---|---|---|---|
| A1 | London–Edinburgh. (St Paul's Cathedral–City boundary). | St Paul's Churchyard (East Side). St Martin le Grand. Aldersgate Street. | .59 | Extension of existing A1 southwards. |
| A3 | London–Portsmouth. (Bank–London Bridge). | King William Street. London Bridge approach. | .33 | Extension of existing A3 northwards. |

| Route number: | Description of Road: | Names of Roads or Streets: | Mileage: | Author's Notes: |
|---|---|---|---|---|
| A4 | London–Bath. (Monument Station–City boundary). | Cannon Street. St Paul's Churchyard (South Side). Ludgate Hill. Ludgate Circus. Fleet Street. | 1.12 | Extension of existing A4 eastwards. |
| A10 | London–King's Lynn. (Bank–Norton Folgate). | Threadneedle Street. Bishopsgate (part). | .73 | Extension of existing A10 southwards. |
| A11 | London–Norwich. (Bank–Whitechapel High Street). | Cornhill. Leadenhall Street. Aldgate. Aldgate High Street. | .67 | Extension of existing A11 westwards. |
| A40 | London–Goodwick. (Bank–Holborn Bars). | Mansion House Street. Poultry. Cheapside. Newgate Street. Holborn Viaduct. Holborn Circus. Holborn. | .98 | Extension of existing A40 eastwards. |
| A100 | London (Monument Station–Tower Hill). | Eastcheap. Great Tower Street (part). Byward Street. | .37 | Extension of existing A100 westwards. |
| A201 | London (Blackfriars Station–Charterhouse Street). | Blackfriars Bridge approach. New Bridge Street. Farringdon Street. | .53 | Centre section within the City boundary, linking the existing separate northern and southern sections. |
| A300 | London (Cheapside–Southwark Bridge). | Queen Street. Southwark Bridge approach. | .27 | Extension of existing A300 northwards. |
| A501 | London (Bank–City boundary). | Princes Street. Moorgate. | .42 | Extension of existing A501 southwards. |
| A1210 | London (Widegate Street–Mansell Street). | Widegate Street (part). Middlesex Street. Mansell Street. | .17 | Newly allocated number. |
| A1211 | London (London Wall–Tower Hill). | London Wall (part). Blomfield Street (part). Liverpool Street. Houndsditch. Minories. | .92 | Newly allocated number. |
| A1212 | London (Fenchurch Street). | Fenchurch Street | .33 | Newly allocated number. |

| Route number: | Description of Road: | Names of Roads or Streets: | Mileage: | Author's Notes: |
|---|---|---|---|---|
| A1213 | London (Monument Station–Threadneedle Street). | Gracechurch Street. Bishopsgate (part). | .25 | Newly allocated number. |
| A3211 | London (Queen Victoria Street, Victoria Embankment). | Queen Victoria Street. Victoria Embankment. | .90 | Eastward extension of existing A3211. |
| A4208 | London (Ludgate Circus–Holborn Circus). | St Bride Street. Shoe Lane (part). St Andrew Street. | .25 | Newly allocated number. |
| | TOTAL MILEAGE OF CLASS I ROADS | | 8.83 | |

| | | | | |
|---|---|---|---|---|
| B100 | London (Farringdon St–City boundary). | Long Lane. Barbican. Beech Street. | .56 | Extension of existing B100 westwards. |
| B128 | London (Aldersgate St–Moorgate). | Gresham Street. Lothbury (part). | .32 | Newly allocated number. |
| B129 | London (Barbican–Moorgate). | Red Cross Street. Fore Street. | .35 | Newly allocated number. |
| B130 | London (Threadneedle St–Liverpool Street). | Old Broad Street. Broad Street. New Broad Street (part). | .26 | Newly allocated number. |
| B131 | London (Lombard Street). | Lombard Street | .15 | Newly allocated number. |
| B132 | London (Queen Victoria Street–Tower Hill). | Upper Thames Street. Lower Thames Street. | 1.04 | Newly allocated number. |
| B133 | London (Monument Street). | Monument Street | .13 | Newly allocated number. |
| B400 | London (Fleet Street–City boundary) | Chancery Lane. | .06 | Extension of existing B400 southwards. |
| B500 | London (Charterhouse Street). | Charterhouse Street. | .31 | Centre section along the City boundary, linking the existing separate western and eastern sections. |
| B501 | London (Newgate Street–City boundary). | St John Street. Lindsay Street. West Smithfield (East side). Little Britain (part). King Edward Street. | .33 | Extension of existing B501 southwards. |
| | TOTAL MILEAGE OF CLASS II ROADS | | 3.51 | |

It is of course difficult to believe that the City's probable classification scheme had not been considered by those who allocated the original numbers in 1922–3. As can be seen from the schedules on pages 60–62, in many cases existing road numbers were simply extended inwards towards the centre of the City.

Something lacking from the scheme shown was a single starting point for the whole national road numbering system. Although the A3 started southwards down King William Street, the A4 started westwards from the A3 but along Cannon Street. The A1 only started its northwards journey from the west end of Cannon Street, going by St Paul's Churchyard (east side), St Martin's le Grand, Aldersgate Street, Goswell Road and Upper Street. The A2 also started elsewhere, actually from the A3 Borough High

Nearly all main thoroughfares in London have road numbers, although it is some time since they were displayed as clearly as this. The photo, taken in June 1941, shows the American radio news correspondent Edward R. Murrow near the BBC's Broadcasting House, from which he beamed his 'This is London' reports to the United States.

63

Road numbers in London and its suburbs have seen significant change. Many have disappeared, such as the A555 Great North Way seen here. Now renumbered the A1, it carries a lot more traffic than seen in this photo of Henly's Corner (where the A1 joins up with and then diverges again from the North Circular Road). The boxy attachment above the sign is a World War Two fitting designed to eliminate glare useful to enemy aircraft. Henly's garage is seen in the background, along with a London Transport trolleybus whose wheel arches have been painted white for greater visibility in the blackout.

Street, at its junction with Great Dover Street. The A5 started from the A4 at Hyde Park Corner, going via Park Lane and the Edgware Road.

As elsewhere, there were significant changes to the numbering system in the City over the years. By the beginning of 1989, very few numbered 'A' roads remained in the City area. These comprised the following only:

**A201** from Blackfriars Bridge northwards along New Bridge Street and Farringdon Road.

**A3211** Victoria Embankment eastwards only as far as Blackfriars Bridge.

**A1210**, that part of Middlesex Street along the City boundary.

**A11** Aldgate High Street and St Botolph Street one-way system.

**A1211** Minories.

*The above were all 'Classified Principal' roads.*

The 'B' roads in the City comprised, in number order:

**B100** from Farringdon Street along West Smithfield, Long Lane, Beech Street, Chiswell Street and Sun Street.

**B128** Gresham Street.

**B130** Old Broad Street.

**B131** Lombard Street.

**B132** Upper Thames Street, Lower Thames Street, Byward Street.

**B133** Monument.

**B400** Chancery Lane.

**B500** Charterhouse Street, south side of Charterhouse Square, Carthusian Street.

**B501** St John Street and Little Britain via Lindsey Street.

The above were all 'Classified Non-Principal' roads.

No other roads had numbers, even though some cartographers have continued to use the old numberings. This is not very helpful, since current policy is not to show road numbers on City signposts. In such a crowded road environment it is thought that travellers find the names of destinations more useful than road numbers.

The present classification and numbering system for roads in the City was introduced in 1989. All the previously mentioned 'B' roads were downgraded to un-numbered roads, with the exception of the B100 stretch along Beech Street, and the B400 down Chancery Lane. There is also still a short stretch of the B500 west of the Farringdon Road, just along the City boundary. With regard to 'Classified Principal' roads, these now run as follows:

**A1** now runs down Goswell Road and Aldersgate Street and St Martin Le Grand.

**A10** now runs down Norton Folgate, Bishopsgate and Gracechuch Street to meet the A3.

**A1211** now runs westwards from Minories via Houndsditch/Dukes Place–Bevis Marks–Camomile Street, Wormwood Street and London Wall.

**A201** remains as before.

**A3** once again runs up to the junction with Cannon Street/Gracechurch Street.

**A300** runs up over Southwark Bridge to the junction with Upper Thames Street.

**A3211** took over the stretch of the B132 mentioned previously, now running right through from the Victoria Embankment as far as Minories (including the roads around Blackfriars Station and the links to the A3.).

**A4** now runs inwards from Strand up Fetter Lane and New Fetter Lane to Holborn.

**A40** now runs along Holborn, Holborn Viaduct and Newgate Street, and includes the link to the A1 at the roundabout with London Wall (this link originally went via Angel Street, which was declassified in 1990 when the new route via Montague Street was newly classified). St Andrew Street, Shoe Lane, St Bride Street and Shoecutter Lane became the A4208.

**A501** now runs down Moorgate but only as far as London Wall.

All other roads remain unnumbered.

# 6
# NUMBERS THAT DON'T ADD UP
## Missing numbers, misplaced roads and other oddities

## Anomalies

Anomalies – or apparent anomalies – abound among British road numbers. The case of Kentish roads north of the A2 numbered A2... instead of A1... has been mentioned already and the A3 is another special case. A Ministry of Transport letter in the National Archives dated 5 February 1937 explains: '... exceptionally, the old Portsmouth Road through Guildford although renumbered remains the boundary between Zones 2 and 3 in order to avoid renumbering of Routes A.31, A.320, A.321 and B.3000 which under altered conditions would otherwise originate in Zone 2.' In fact the Guildford Bypass was actually allocated a route number of A3100 on 14 July 1934, pending completion of the whole bypass. When work was finished, the numbers were swapped over, the A3 becoming the new bypass route and the A3100 the old road through Guildford, Godalming and Milford.

## Swaps

Swaps occur where two roads exchange identities. For any motorist using an outdated road atlas this kind of change can be highly confusing, such as north of Oxford where the old A43 has taken on the number A34 and the old A34 is now the A44. Another swap occurred north of Purley where the A22 became the A23 and vice versa. Old maps show the A22 continuing northwards and the A23 from the south terminating there, whereas today the situation is reversed with the A22 truncated to allow the A23 to continue to Westminster.

## Splits

A growing trend in recent years has been to break up established A-roads, renumbering one or more intermediate sections, presumably to dissuade motorists from using them for long journeys but rather to encourage them to take an alternative route along motorways or other less congested highways. Some of these are now so hopelessly separated that a newcomer would not recognise them as a once-contiguous route and to be fair, most travellers would not use both parts in one journey.

The SABRE group website cites two classic 'splits': the A34 (Winchester–Oxford and Birmingham–Manchester) and the A74 (two five mile-long roads in different countries nearly 100 miles apart). Other non-contiguous roads include the A741, severed by the River Clyde and the Renfrew Ferry and the A46 (Tewkesbury–Coventry and Leicester–Lincoln). Across the country many more such examples can be found.

## Realigned routes and re-used numbers

The A34 just mentioned is a case where an established thoroughfare has been chopped and changed out of all recognition. Another is the A45, which for many years ran from Birmingham to the East Coast port of Felixstowe. Since then its route has been altered radically in recognition of new traffic flows. The construction first of the M6 motorway and then of the A14 M1–A1 Link Road relegated the status of the western part of the A45, whilst the growing importance of Felixstowe as a container port demanded the upgrading of the eastern section. East of Wellingborough the A45 has been diverted and it now terminates at a junction with the present A14 (formerly A604) near Thrapston. The old route of the A45 from Higham Ferrers to Cambridge has been downgraded to B645 as far as St Neots, becoming the A428 from there to Cambridge. Skirting Cambridge the new A14 assumes the general route of the old A45 and continues under this new identity to Felixstowe.

The present A14 has been rebuilt throughout but takes the number of the old A14, which ran from Royston to Huntingdon and is now the A1198. The section of the new A14 from Alconbury to Godmanchester is the only part that follows the route of the old A14.

## Doubles

'Doubles' in roader-speak are road numbers that exist simultaneously in two parts of the country, created presumably through accidental duplication. A good example is the A594, on the one hand the Leicester inner ring road or alternatively the main route between Maryport and Cockermouth in Cumbria. Another is the A1114, which exists both in Gateshead and at Great Barrow on a suburban route around the southern side of Chelmsford.

Another case of duplication involves roads on St Mary's, the largest of the Scilly Isles; the A3112 there has a counterpart at Melksham, Wiltshire. Not two but three roads bear the number B198. One is in fenland country near Wisbech, Cambridgeshire whilst the other two (and they are two separate roads) are in Cheshunt, Hertfordshire. Another kind of double occurs in Reading, where the A329(M) runs parallel to, but a distance from, the old A329. Logically the newer road should be the M329 because having two separate roads with the same number is officially taboo.

## Misfits

Misfits are road numbers outside their own proper zone and a prime example is the A3400, which begins Junction 4 of the M42 and heads south to meet the A44 near Chipping Norton. Although bearing a Zone 3 number, its entire length is within Zone 4. The apparent misnumbering is explained, if not justified, by the fact that the A3400 is a renumbered remnant of the old A34 road, which began in Zone 3. Another apparent anomaly is the A41, which starts east of the A1 and thus in Zone 1. Originally, however, the road started west of the A1, in Zone 4.

## Records

A number of claims have been made for the UK's shortest numbered road, with some citing the 150 yards-long B500 in London as the winner. B roads in the City of London lost their numbers in 1989, however, making the best claimant the B5233 (St Annes Road East) in Lytham at just over a mile long.

Another source of harmless amusement is identifying the furthest separation of locations on two sequential road numbers. Examples cited include from the A598 in Golders Green, north London to the A597 in Workington (307 miles), from Harwich on the A136 to Eaglescliff on the A135 (268 miles) and Billericay on the A176 to Stockton on the A177 (260 miles). No doubt many other similar journeys could be construed!

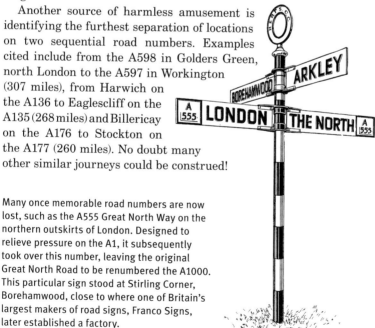

Many once memorable road numbers are now lost, such as the A555 Great North Way on the northern outskirts of London. Designed to relieve pressure on the A1, it subsequently took over this number, leaving the original Great North Road to be renumbered the A1000. This particular sign stood at Stirling Corner, Borehamwood, close to where one of Britain's largest makers of road signs, Franco Signs, later established a factory.

# Missing numbers

A fascinating pursuit is the search for missing junction numbers, such as Junction 3 of the M1 motorway. In fact the junction does exist, in use for

Substitute roads normally assume the number of the routes they replace but this was not the practice when London's new arterial roads were constructed. The A41 through Hendon and Mill Hill first had the ungainly number of A5088, whilst the Barnet Bypass was originally christened the equally unmemorable A5092, later becoming the A555 and finally A1. The A555 still exists today but has been assigned to an airport link road in Manchester.

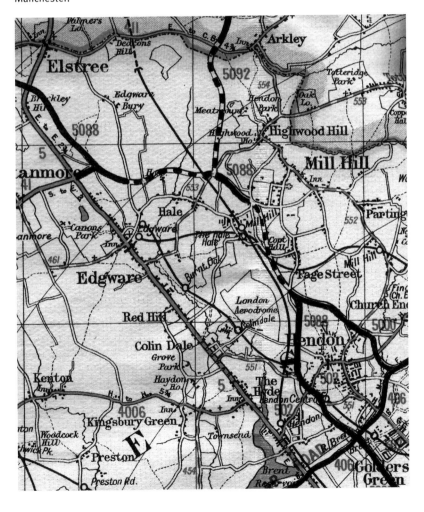

access to Scratchwood (London Gateway) Services. However, its intended main function was a connection to the A1 but this link was never built, probably as it would have defiled the Scratchwood urban park and picnic ground. The number M125 has been suggested if the link had been built as a proper spur motorway.

## Roads with no goal

Highways that lead nowhere are more common than supposed; some are related to features that were never built, whilst others serve establishments that no longer exist. Some people imagine the numerous incomplete slip roads leading from Britain's motorways were built in preparation for secret government boltholes for the protection of senior officials in times of grave national emergency. This is of course a myth and the majority of these were intended merely for motorway service areas that were never in fact built (some of these facilities are even shown as 'planned' on early maps of the motorway system).

'Secret' motorway junctions do exist but tend to have very prosaic uses. Some lead to depots where road surface materials and winter salt are stored. Another, roughly halfway between junctions 14 (Milton Keynes) and 15 (Northampton south) on the M1 serves a dive-under tunnel that enables emergency service vehicles to cross over to the opposite carriageway. Two other junctions barred to the public are on the M4 (serving a munitions base) and on the M11 (for a security printing works).

A subject of speculation is the broadened central reservation of the M25 immediately east of the A1 crossing at junction 23 (Bignell's Corner, South Mimms). This was provided for a never-built junction from which a new motorway spur would head in a south-westerly direction to join the M1 at junction 3.

Some roads appear to serve no function, such as the short M45 spur from the M1 to the A45 at Dunchurch. Its raison d'être lies in the fact that the M1 originally had a north-westerly trajectory and was christened the London-Birmingham motorway. To save construction of a motorway all the way into Birmingham the existing A45 road was upgraded to dual carriageway from Dunchurch for much of the route into Birmingham. The M1 itself ended just north at Crick, where the A5 trunk road was upgraded with several dual carriageway sections north thereof.

A very substantial (but un-numbered) road leads from the A6 north of Bedford to the former Royal Aircraft Establishment research station at Thurleigh. In addition, just south of Thurleigh, a narrow country lane still suddenly splits into two carriageways as it passes through a dip where a never-built aircraft taxiway from the former RAF Thurleigh airfield to Twinwoods aerodrome was due to have passed across.

# Defunct highways

Many roads have disappeared from a numbering point of view after being absorbed into other routes. The A42 mentioned earlier is a case in point. More unusually some A roads have swapped identity with motorways, and vice versa. Notable cases include two sections of the M25 motorway that opened ahead of the completed route. The first section of the proposed M16 from current junction 23 to 25 opened as an all-traffic road under the designation A1178 and later took the number A1005 before finally becoming the M25. The section between junctions 17 and 19 opened as the A405 in 1975 at a time when the eventual route of the M25 south of junction 17 was yet to be decided. When the M25 between junctions 16 and 17 finally opened ten years later the green A405 signs were changed for blue ones, a few days after the motorway actually opened.

The converse also happens, such as the M41 in west London downgraded to become the A3220 and the A40(M) nearby now more simply the A40. Part of the A329(M) near Winnersh, Berks. is now the A3290. These

Most of the 'mystery' incomplete junctions on Britain's motorways have their origins in service areas that were planned but never built (and not in the secret government facilities that conspiracy theorists like to imagine). Lutterworth and Stretton-Under-Fosse seen on this map of 1970 are two of these long-forgotten projects.

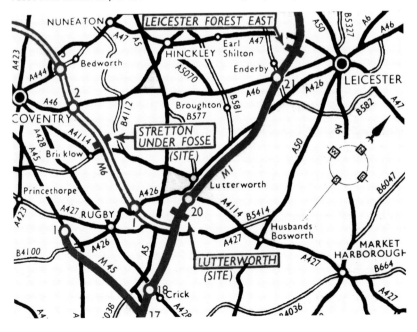

motorway disappearances are the result of administrative alterations but there are also a number of routes that have disappeared physically. These include roads made redundant and motorway junctions eliminated following replacement by superior facilities elsewhere.

## The archaeology of new roads

Although prehistoric remains can last thousands of years, some new road constructions disappear almost without trace in three decades or less. A prime example is the old A74 at Beattock and just north of Lockerbie to a point south of Lesmahagow. Upgraded to a dual carriageway in 1973, it was later supplanted by the motorway-standard A74(M) but a number of stretches remain fossilised in a kind of time warp. Parts have been renumbered A701, B7076 and B7078, with one of the two carriageways landscaped into invisibility. Keen-eyed road archaeologists will spot an abandoned filling station, the foundations of a Little Chef rest stop and a bus stop pole far removed from the roadside where a pull-in has been seeded over. A well-illustrated article can be found on the CBRD website.

Motorway junctions that have been superseded include the original southern terminal of the M1 at Mill Hill (still visible to those with sharp eyes) and the first M4 junction for Windsor (now almost completely removed). This was a junction with the A308 at Holyport, then numbered Junction 8, whilst the Junction 9 of that time is now numbered 9A on the A404(M). When the M4 was widened and extended to Reading and beyond, the old Junction 8 was closed (the extension began very close to this point). The A308(M) spur was built to maintain the old connection, whilst the old alignment of the M4 became the A423(M), later renumbered again to A404(M) when the M40 extension to Birmingham was opened and the old A423 lost its trunk status.

# 7
# BRITAIN'S OTHER NUMBERED ROADS
## Milton Keynes, Euroroutes and other odd numbers

The only theme that unites the subjects of this chapter is that they have no logical place in any other section. So without further ado we make our way to Britain's most radical new city to begin this journey of discovery.

## The grid system of Milton Keynes

As well as concrete cows, Milton Keynes is provided with an innovative road numbering scheme that was introduced at an early stage of its planning. This local numbering system applies only to the new-build area (the remainder of Milton Keynes incorporates the existing towns of Bletchley, Wolverton and Newport Pagnell as well as a number of ancient villages). Using 'H' and 'V' prefixes (for 'horizontal' and 'vertical' routes on the map respectively), the scheme provides effectively a grid of roads with numbers progressing incrementally to ease direction finding. This is in addition to the local 'A' and 'B' numbering system and both systems appear on signs and local maps. The 'V' roads are numbered consecutively from west to east and the 'H' roads are numbered consecutively from north to south, although strictly speaking the grid is neither geometric nor aligned exactly with the points of the compass. The numbering range, which has not been incremented for several years, runs from H1 to H10 and from V1 to V11.

## Trunk Road Routes

For the sake of completeness we must mention also the UK Trunk Road route numbers. These were used by the Ministry of Transport for administrative convenience in schedules published as attachments to the various Trunk Roads Acts of 1936 to 1946. The numbered long-distance routes embraced several individual road numbers and should be seen as reference designations for legislative and planning purposes. They had no relevance to drivers and did not appear on signs or in other documents. It appears they were dropped following enactment of the Highways Act 1959.

## 'E' numbers: the Euroroutes

In mainland Europe a system of through route numbering of roads that traverse national borders was introduced many years ago, under the United Nations Economic Commission for Europe. This system employs the letter E followed by the route number and is used widely on maps and signs on the Continent. Contrary to widely held belief, the scheme has nothing to do with the European Union and long pre-dates it.

The register of routes has been restructured completely at least once and is still being updated under the auspices of the United Nations Economic Commission for Europe (UNECE). The original numbering scheme has been abandoned and numbers, which now run into the 900s, follow a pattern of even numbers for east-west roads and odd numbers for roads running north-south.

In Britain the enthusiasm for adding new numbers to the older established numbering system was never strong and the E numbers are shown on very few maps of British origin. Although plans were drawn up to show the E-number on motorway signs (in a green patch alongside the existing M-number), they were abandoned in 1994 (older readers may recall that

On this map of the Maidstone area produced for military intelligence purposes in 1982 by the Soviet General Staff, the pan-European number (E107, no longer in use) precedes the M2 motorway's national identity. Few British maps ever showed these E numbers.

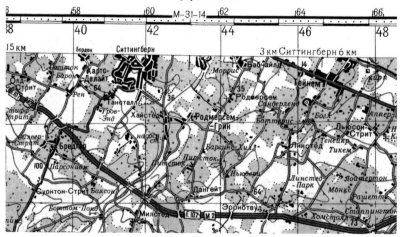

trunk road direction signs to ports had a green background back in the 1950s). The European Union is also developing a Trans-European Road Network, and this might be extended to include re-numbering of some of the UK's roads at some time in the future.

Although E numbers have never been shown generally on British direction signs, one did appear in 1999, in connection with the Tall Ships Race in Greenock. A spot of inspired exuberance led to an 'E5' Euroroute sign being erected on the A8. Several destinations were listed, the furthest being Algeciras, making a strange sight on a British road sign of a four-figure mileage.

## Table of current Euroroutes in Britain, adapted from an original by Martyn Hix

| Euroroute number | UK and Eire terminal points | UK route details | Continental route |
|---|---|---|---|
| E1 179 miles, 286km | Lisburn, Northern Ireland to Wexford, Eire. | Via A1, N1, M1, N1, N11, M11 and N11. | The E1 runs also in Europe from La Coruna, Spain to Seville, Spain. |
| E5 467 miles, 747km | Portsmouth to Greenock. | Via A3, M275, M27, M3, A34, M40, M42, M6, A74 and A74(M), M74, M73, M8 and A8. | The E5 runs also in Europe from Le Havre, France to Malaga, Spain. |
| E13 173 miles, 277km | M25 Junction 21, to M621, Leeds. | Via M1. | |
| E15 738 miles, 1181km | Dover to Wick. | Via A20, M20, M25/ E30, A282, M25, A1M and A1, A720, A8, A902, A90, M90, A9 and A99. | The E15 runs also in Europe from Calais, France to Malaga, Spain. |
| E16 52 miles, 83km | Londonderry, Northern Ireland to M2/E18 (Antrim), Northern Ireland. | Via A6 and M22. | The E16 runs also in Europe in Norway from Bergen to Sandvika. |
| E18 189 miles, 302km | Lisburn, Northern Ireland to Newcastle-upon-Tyne. | Via M1, A12, M2/E16, A8, ferry, A75, A74/ E5, A69, A68 and A69. | The E18 runs also in Europe from Kristiansand, Norway to St Petersburg, Russia. |
| E20 275 miles, 440km | Hull (ferry terminal) to Ennis, Eire. | Via A1033, A63, M62, A5080, A5047, (ferries via Isle of Man), N7, M7, N7, M7, N7, N18. | The E20 runs also in Europe from Esbjerg, Denmark to St Petersburg, Russia. |

| Euroroute number | UK and Eire terminal points | UK route details | Continental route |
|---|---|---|---|
| E22 235 miles, 376km | Holyhead (ferry terminal) to Grimsby. | Via A5, A55, A494, A550, A5117, (M6/M56 junction then follows E5/M6 and E20/M62 to M62 J35), M18, M180 and A180. | The E22 runs also in Europe from Amsterdam, Netherlands to Norkopping, Sweden. |
| E24 112 miles, 179km | Northampton to Ipswich. | Via A45, A428, A421, A1, A428, (Cambridge), A14, A11 and A14. | |
| E30 480 miles, 768km | Felixstowe to Cork (Eire). | Via A14, A12, M25/E15, A282/E15, M25, M4, A48, A40, Fishguard-Rosslare ferry, N25 and N8. | The E30 runs also in Europe from The Hague, Netherlands to Moscow, Russia. |
| E32 16 miles, 26km | Harwich to Colchester. | Via A120. | |
| E201 100 miles, 160km | Blackrock (Eire) to Portlaoise (Eire). | Via N8. | |

The above table is markedly different from that of 40 years ago. At this time routes numbered E1 to E25 were main international highways, with branch and link roads numbered from E30 to E106:

## Table of Euroroutes in Britain, as in 1962

| Euroroute number | UK and Eire terminal points | UK route details | Continental route |
|---|---|---|---|
| E1 | Southampton (ferry terminal) to London. | Via A31. | The E1 ran also in Europe from Le Havre, France to Palermo in Italy. |
| E2 | Dover (ferry terminal) to London. | Via A20. | The E2 ran also in Europe from Calais, France to Brindisi, Italy. |
| E31 | London to Glasgow. | Via A5, A50, A43, A1, A66, A6, A74. | |
| E32 | Abington (E31) to Edinburgh. | A73. | |

| Euroroute number | UK and Eire terminal points | UK route details | Continental route |
|---|---|---|---|
| E33 | Northampton (E31) to Liverpool. | A45, A34, A51 | |
| E34 | Cannock (E33) to Holyhead. | A5 | |
| E5 | Dover (ferry terminal) to London. | Via A20. | The E5 ran also in Europe from Calais, France to Istanbul and the Turkish-Syrian border. |
| E8 | Harwich (ferry terminal) to London. | Via A120, A12. | The E8 ran also in Europe from the Hook of Holland to Warsaw, Poland and the USSR. |

# Essential Service Routes

The military uses of motorways began with Hitler's autobahns, some of which doubled as emergency airstrips. The motorway era began later in Britain and almost as soon as it did, the strategic functions of motorways were not overlooked. Beginning in the Cold War years of the 1960s, in the event of a 'civil emergency' or war, motorways and other major roads would be reclassified as 'Essential Service Routes' (ESRs) reserved for military use only. In a state of contingency, checkpoints would be established at each junction by the police to prevent use by refugees and other civilians.

In his book *War Plan UK* published in 1982, author Duncan Campbell describes ESRs as a co-ordinated network of major roads that would be kept clear for essential traffic. The A and M numbers of the roads and motorways were not modified under this scheme and the book includes several maps showing the routes designated as ESRs. In the greater London area a number of radial routes and ring roads were selected as ESRs and in this case they were assigned special numbers, however, as follows:

| ESR designation | Equivalent to |
|---|---|
| ESR 1 | A30 |
| ESR 1A | M4 |
| ESR 2 | M40 via A40 |
| ESR 3 | M1 |
| ESR 4 | A1 |
| ESR 4A | A1081 link from A1 to ESR Route 'B' |

Britain's trunk roads played a vital strategic role during the Second World War and were expected to do the same in any subsequent conflict in the Cold War era. Seen here is a wartime 'cowled' direction sign made by GEC Ltd, with a special hood and angle of illumination to eliminate all glare and light spill under black-out conditions.

| ESR designation | Equivalent to |
|---|---|
| ESR 5 | A10 |
| ESR 6 | A11 |
| ESR 7 | A127 via A12 |
| ESR 7A | A12 |
| ESR 8 | A13 |
| ESR 9 | M2 via A2 |
| ESR 10 | M20 via A20 |
| ESR 11 | A21 |
| ESR 11A | A223 link between A20 and A21 |
| ESR 12 | A23 via A22 |
| ESR 13 | A24 via A217 |
| ESR 14 | A3 |

| ESR Route 'A' | Peacetime inner ring road (A406/A205) |
|---|---|
| ESR Route 'AA' | Blackwall Tunnel and access roads |
| ESR Route 'B' | Outer ring road route including A110, A121, A123, A1112, A13, A282, A2, A223, A232, A240, A3, A309, A308, A311, A312, A409, A410, A41, A411, A1000, A110. |
| ESR Route 'C' or Constabulary Ring Road | A25 and other roads |

Campbell mentions also another version of this scheme known as the Military Road Route System (MRRS), which is smaller and overlaps ESRs to a large extent. His book includes a map of the routes, each of which is named after an animal, such as STAG, ELK, CAT, HEN, DOG, BUCK and PIG. These roads are effectively a 'preferred' set of routes for use by military convoys and troop movements, in peacetime as well as war.

Incidentally the notion of using motorways as airstrips is not unknown in Britain. Before the M63 opened in the mid-1970s some newspapers printed a picture of a Jaguar bomber taking off from the carriageway near the USAF airfield at Burtonwood.

## Hospitals

Before leaving this chapter we must mention the basement of Addenbrooke's Hospital in Cambridge, which has road-type junction numbers in the subterranean service corridors. These are used largely by tug trucks that ferry materials around the vast site, in which junction numbering makes eminent sense. The Royal Infirmary in Derby goes one better and publishes on its website a map of the hospital for visitors. The corridors all have motorway-style junction numbers (from J1 to J20, including J8a, J10a and J10b)!

Not all of Britain's road network was numbered, in particular the private road systems of industrial users. This publicity photo shows the driving school network parallel to the main A4 road just west of Taplow station. It was opened by the Great Western Railway in early 1939 "for the instruction of recruits to the motor-driving staff" and included road junctions and a steep hill. For many years the railway even had its own driving test examiners, who were authorised to pass or fail new drivers.

# 8
# ISLANDS AND IRELAND
## Trunks, Links and other exotic delights

## BRITISH ISLANDS

### The Isle of Man

In 1923, the Isle of Man Highway and Transport Board commissioned an independent report from the Ministry of Transport into the condition of the Island's roads. Mr A.J. Lyddon, O.B.E., A.M.I.C.E. who was then Divisional Road Engineer (Northern) Ministry of Transport, carried out the survey. In the same year, Francis G. Cornish, M.I.M.&CtyE was appointed Surveyor General on the Island, having previously been Assistant County Surveyor for Devonshire. In his first annual report to the Board in May 1924, he made reference to 1st, 2nd and 3rd class roads, but no numbering system had been applied by that time.

R.C.W. Brown, M.I.C.&MunE, was appointed to the post of Surveyor General on 31 March 1930, having previously been Divisional Surveyor Eastern on the Island. Brown was too old to serve in the armed forces during the Second World War, but was therefore able to catch up on a variety of administrative tasks for the island government. Little work was carried out on the roads during the war, but some work on rural roads and on drainage trenches was carried out using internees. Brown drew up the basis of all the rights of way on the Island and listed all the public roads that existed at that time. These were then designated as Class 1, Class 2, Class 3 or Unscheduled Public Roads and duly numbered with the Class 1 roads radiating from Douglas. The first official record of this system was a schedule attached to the Highway (Unadopted Roads) Act 1953.

It was only in the early 1960s that the roads were then designated alphanumerically, as in the UK, largely influenced by Charles A. Lake A.M.I.C.E., M.I.MunE., who followed R.C. Brown as Surveyor General when he retired on 30 September 1959. Lake had been Divisional Surveyor for Perth and Kinross Joint County Council before coming to the Island and was therefore familiar with the UK system. The Island's road numbering now followed Brown's system, but replacing Class 1 with 'A', Class 2 with 'B' and so on. These designations were placed on Ordnance Survey maps from then on.

The Isle of Man's numbering system, like that of the mainland, starts with the A1 running north-west from Douglas to Peel. The A2 runs from Douglas to Ramsey, the A3 from Ramsey to Castletown, the A4 from Peel to Kirk Michael and the A5 from Douglas to Port Erin via Castletown. The 'A' road numbers continue on into double-digit numbers up to the A47 (some of these roads, like the A8 and A33 for example, are only very short lengths of road in the north of the Island and Douglas respectively). However, there are no sectors as on the mainland. The 'B' roads also start from 1 and have single and double-digit numbers in sequence up to the B82, thus meaning that the first 47 numbers exist as both 'A' and 'B' roads, although these are not usually in close proximity to one another. The 'A' and 'B' roads form most of the network of roads on the island, leaving a much smaller length of other roads in the country areas, and those in the main towns. These other roads on the island are 'C', 'D' and 'E' roads and also 'U' roads, the latter of which are unscheduled and unmade. The 'F' designation is also used for footpaths, although some of these are along the routes of much older trackways. Designations other than 'A' or 'B' are not normally shown on signposts.

The roads in the Isle of Man are currently the responsibility of the Highways Division of the Department of Transport, which is part of the Isle of Man government. They, like the mainland, raise taxes, including vehicle excise, that can be used for the repair and maintenance of the Island's road network. They do not receive any external funding from anyone else!

## The Isle of Wight

Roads on the Isle of Wight are presently the responsibility of the Isle of Wight Council, a unitary authority set up on 1 April 1995. Before this, the Isle of Wight County Council was the highway authority for the island, although there were also two borough councils in operation. The island simply comes within sector 3 and all 'A' and 'B' road numbers thus begin with 3. All the numbers have four digits.

## The Isles of Scilly

The Council of the Isles of Scilly is actually one of the oldest unitary authorities in the country. Some form of classification was applied to the roads in the island of St. Mary's, such as they were, around 1919. Yet until 1972, there were actually no hard-surfaced roads on the island. In 1972 construction of the island's main road network began and there are now both 'A' and 'B' roads on the island. Since the islands all come within sector 3, all the road numbers, not surprisingly, begin with a 3. The three classified 'A' roads are numbered A3110 (a roughly circular route around the centre of the island), A3111 and A3112. There are also three classified 'B' roads, but surprisingly, these have never been allocated numbers.

## The Orkney Islands

This island group off the north-east coast of Scotland comprises 70 islands, of which only 18 are inhabited. Of the inhabited islands, only Mainland, South Ronaldsay, Hoy, Shapinsay, Stronsay, Rousay, Eday, Sanday and Westray have 'A' or 'B' roads (all but the first two have 'B' roads only). All these islands simply come within sector 9 and all 'A' and 'B' road numbers thus start with 9. The 'A' road numbers are all three-digit numbers and the 'B' road numbers are all four-digit numbers. Many of the 'B' roads are narrow roads with passing places. The present highway authority for the Orkney Islands is the Department of Technical Services, Orkney Islands Council. There is no local numbering system for roads other than the 'A' or 'B' roads, but all the smaller roads do have names to distinguish them.

## The Shetland Islands

This island group, also off the north-east coast of Scotland comprises 100 islands, of which only 15 are inhabited. Of the inhabited islands, only Mainland, Yell, Unst and Fetlar have 'A' or 'B' roads (Fetlar has only one 'B' road). All these islands also come within sector 9 and all 'A' and 'B' road numbers therefore start with a 9. The 'A' road numbers are all three-digit numbers and the 'B' road numbers are all four-digit numbers. The A968 also continues on three separate islands with vehicle ferries linking the separate sections. Many of the 'B' roads are narrow roads with passing places. The Shetland Islands Council, a unitary authority, is the present highway authority. This replaced the Zetland County Council and the Lerwick Town Council in the early 1970s. There are a number of 'C' roads on the islands, but these are very few and remain in single digit numbers. Other roads are all numbered and are usually prefixed with the letter 'U', but some lists of the smaller roads have also used an 'X' prefix at some time in the past.

## The Western Isles or Outer Hebrides

This island group off the west coast of Scotland stretches for some 130 miles, from the tiny island of Berneray in the south, to the main Isle of Lewis in the north. South Uist, Benbecula, North Uist and Harris/Isle of Lewis (the last two of which comprise one large island) all have 'A' and 'B' roads. All these islands come within sector 8 and all 'A' and 'B' road numbers thus start with 8. The 'A' roads all have three-digit numbers and the 'B' roads have either three- or four-digit numbers. The tiny island of

Barra, almost at the southern end of the island group, has only one 'A' road, numbered A888, which goes right around the island in a roughly circular shape! (That particular number did not exist in the original scheme of 1922–3 however.) The Comhairle Nan Eilean Siar (Western Isles Council) is the present highway authority for the islands. There are also a number of 'C' roads on the islands. These use numbers from 30–50, 78, 79, 116, 117 and 118. Unusually, there is an agreement for some heavy goods vehicles (which do not leave the islands) not to need a tax disc!

# THE CHANNEL ISLANDS

## The island of Jersey

The Public Services Department of the States of Jersey is presently responsible for the roads on the island. It appoints a Public Services Committee to act as the highway authority and this committee receives a budget from the States of Jersey, allocated from general taxation income. There is no road fund licence as such on the island (it was abolished some years ago) but there is a tax on petrol. The Committee looks after all the 'A', 'B' and 'C' roads, but the island's 12 Parishes administer the smaller roads or lanes. The latter are often narrow lanes that would not have a white line down the centre. It is the law that Parishes must name all these smaller roads or lanes so that they are easily identifiable. They do not have a separate series of numbers allocated as might happen elsewhere in the UK for example.

On the island of Jersey, the classification scheme appears to be slightly different from elsewhere. Main road numbers are prefixed with 'A' and 'B'. 'A' road numbers run from the A1–A17 inclusive. The A1, A2 and A4 roughly hug the southern and south-eastern coastline and the A3 and A5–A13 roughly radiate from St Helier or the A1 in an anti-clockwise direction in numerical order (apart from the A3 which seems out of sequence?). The 'B' roads are numbered from the B21 to the B92 inclusive. Jersey also has Secondary Roads that are given 'C' prefixed numbers, which start from the C93 and end with the C125 (all numbers in this range are used). Unusually, these are shown and numbered on Ordnance Survey maps and there are instances where these 'C' numbers also appear on the road signs themselves. The choice of an 'A', 'B' or 'C' classification appears to have been dictated by the number of vehicles using the road, whether the road is a bus route, or if it links important centres of population on the island.

It is thought that the numbering system was devised and introduced by Cyril Warren in the 1940s. Warren worked in the then States Engineers

Department (later the Public Works Department) and was in the department during the period of occupation by the Germans. Some road construction did take place in the north of the island during the occupation, and Warren was involved in this as well.

## The island of Guernsey

The island of Guernsey is administered by the States of Guernsey. Responsibility for roads falls into two categories. Firstly, there is the Public Thoroughfares Committee, which looks after road maintenance, re-surfacing and sewers. Then there is the States Traffic Committee, which looks after any road improvements together with safety and signs/white lines. These bodies are funded from general taxation including road tax, voted to them by the Island's Treasury.

Guernsey is smaller than Jersey and has no 'main' or 'secondary' roads. Some earlier maps of the island do, however, show three different classes of roads, but these were put there really just to highlight the main routes for the benefit of tourists. Surprisingly, there is no road numbering system of any kind on the island, not even for internal purposes. The Traffic Committee does use a hierarchy for the classification of roads, dependent largely on the level of traffic using them. This is divided into four categories:

1. Special Route (the one inter-harbour route)
2. Traffic Priority Routes
3. Local Circulation Routes
4. Neighbourhood Roads (lanes without footpaths, some of which also have no names). There are also some estate roads but these are not usually looked after by the State.

Up until about 20 years ago, there were almost no road signs on the island, as the locals knew where they were going and did not need them! But as tourism has grown and the level of foreign vehicles visiting increased, there was a need to have at least some direction signs and these have been slowly appearing since.

## The island of Alderney

Alderney has its own local authority, the States of Alderney who look after the small road network.

## Sark, Herm and Jethou

Sark has no tarmac roads and no motorised vehicles other than tractors. Herm has no motor vehicles either, but does have one length of tarmacadamed road, albeit subject to little wear! Jethou only has one house on it and no roads to speak of.

# ROAD CLASSIFICATION AND NUMBERING IN IRELAND

The Grand Jury Act of 1765 in Ireland abolished statute labour and established the post of a local surveyor responsible for roads. Surprisingly, these Grand Juries could take land for new roads without resorting to Parliament. There were also many toll trusts that did not end until about 1845. The first toll trust in Ireland was established in 1729 for the Dublin to Kilcullen Road.

With the passing of the Local Government (Ireland) Act of 1898, thirty-three County Councils (two in Tipperary) were established, together with the County Boroughs of Belfast, Cork, Dublin, Limerick, Londonderry and Waterford. Boroughs and Urban District Councils were also set up at the same time. The same Act made these Local Authorities the 'Road Authorities' for all public roads. It also provided for 'Main Roads' to be identified (the various Councils could decide which roads were 'Main Roads') and these would be the responsibility of the County Councils. The County Councils were also responsible for half of the costs of maintenance for 'Main Roads', the other half being levied on the district. Where 'Main Roads' passed through Borough and Urban District Council areas, the Borough and UDCs had the say over what monies were to be expended. (The right to take land for new roads without resort to Parliament was removed by the 1898 Act, as the same right had not existed on the mainland.)

On 1 May 1899, General Order 173 came into effect and provided for the 'Main Roads' to be declared. (This order was rescinded later on and replaced by Order No. 304 of 17 February 1909.) But not every county decided to declare 'Main Roads'. The County Council of Monaghan went so far as to declare that there should be 'no main roads' in the county. Fourteen other counties also decided not to have any main roads.

The Road Board that had been brought into being under the 1909 Act had separate committees for Ireland and Scotland. Although it only dealt with a relatively small mileage of principal roads in Ireland, that were called 'National' or 'Trunk' roads, grants were paid totalling £637,218 up to when the Road Board ceased to exist.

The Ministry of Transport Act of 1919 gave the Minister power to classify roads as he thought fit and eventually, as has been noted previously, three separate categories were established – Class I roads; Class II roads; Unclassified roads. Many traffic counts and surveys had been carried out to justify which roads were of the most importance. In Ireland, a preliminary schedule of roads to be classified had been prepared, largely based on the earlier 'Main Road' network.

But whilst the Road Board's powers had been transferred to the

Minister of Transport on the mainland in 1919, the same was not true for Ireland. The old Road Board's powers were transferred to the Local Government Board. Further changes took place on 1 January 1920, when an Order in Council transferred various powers and duties in respect of roads from the Local Government Board to the Ministry of Transport. These changes did not take effect until 26 April 1920, when the Minister of Transport took over powers in relation to various modes of transport, but including: 'Roads, Bridges and Ferries, and Vehicles and Traffic thereon'. The Ministry then sent an Assistant Director of Roads to Ireland (with an office in Dublin) and he worked there for about 18 months.

As from 1 December 1921, the Minister of Transport's powers in respect of Northern Ireland were transferred to the government of Northern Ireland. Later, on 1 April 1922, the financial responsibilities and powers in respect of Southern Ireland were transferred to the government of Southern Ireland under the Government of Ireland Act of 1920. They in turn gave them to the new Department of Local Government and Public Health.

## Northern Ireland

In Northern Ireland, a scheme of road classification was prepared and adopted in consultation with the highway authorities, much as had been done on the mainland. A separate numbering system, but using similar A and B prefixes for the different classes as on the mainland, was also used. The exact origins of this system are not known, but the similarity to that on the mainland is notable. The A1 runs from Belfast south to the border between Newry and Dundalk (it then meets the N1 – see page 88 – which continues south to Dublin). The A2 runs around the northern coastline to Londonderry. However, there are no sectors as on the mainland, so the other numbers are seemingly allocated in an arbitrary way. Because the B roads are numbered from B1, there are many instances where both A and B roads (sometimes in the same proximity) have the same number. The borders of Northern Ireland are the extremities of that system.

The Roads Act of 1920 that had abolished the Road Board and the Road Improvement Fund had established in its place a Road Fund for Northern Ireland. The purpose of this fund was to assist in the maintenance and improvement of the roads. The Fund's administration was passed to the Ministry of Home Affairs and later to the Ministry of Commerce.

In 1937, an Act was passed that allowed the Ministry of Commerce to construct new roads and then pass these to the local authority areas through which they passed for future maintenance, with assistance from the Road Fund. One such road was the Belfast to Holywood by-pass road, which had been partly completed before World War Two caused work to stop.

A further Roads Act was passed by the Northern Ireland Parliament in 1948. This established a Trunk Road System, similar to the arrangements on the mainland. The Ministry of Commerce now became the road authority for these highways, comprising some 350 miles as at 1 April 1949.

## Republic of Ireland

The period 1919–22 had been a difficult one in Ireland with two 'governments' in operation – the Sinn Fein Parliament and the UK Parliament. Section 17(3) of the Ministry of Transport Act, 1919, made specific provision to only give road grants in Ireland to those counties that would accept them from the UK government (i.e. recognise that authority).

Whilst by 1922, many counties had declared 'Main Roads', 14 had not yet done so. But no system of classification had been introduced, although much preparatory work had been done. Details of the provisional classification were set out in the report of the Department of Local Government and Public Health for the years 1922–25. This refers to Class I roads as 'Trunk Roads' and Class II roads as 'Link Roads'. The origin of these terms is unclear, but the new administration may have wished to be deliberately different to the system adopted in Great Britain and Northern Ireland.

In fact the Republic's original classification system was really only slightly different to that of the UK. Main roads (the equivalent of our A roads) were prefixed with the letter T and occasionally had branches off them, suffixed with the letter A. The roads of lesser importance (the equivalent of our B roads) were prefixed with the letter L and occasionally also had branches off them, suffixed with the letter A. Unlike the UK, the Republic's L roads had one, two or three digit numbers, whereas our B roads have only three or four digit numbers. There were therefore instances where a T and an L road had the same number and might have been in close proximity. As has been mentioned, 'T' stood for Trunk and 'L' for Link. It is worth noting that the T1, T2, T3, T4, T5, T6 and T7 did radiate roughly from Dublin in a clockwise direction, although they did not all actually start within the capital itself, nor did they give rise to sectors in the same way as in the UK.

## National Roads

By the 1960s, the Department of Local Government was considering the re-classification of roads on a functional basis. In 1963, a nationwide traffic census was carried out as the first main step in this long-running process. The same year saw the adoption of a network of 'Arterial Roads' (mostly radiating from Dublin) and special improvement grants were allocated to these routes. The classification system eventually adopted included National Roads (National Primary and National Secondary) and Regional Roads (Regional Primary and Regional Secondary). By 1969, a network of 1,500 miles of national primary roads and 1,500 miles of national secondary roads had been announced. These national roads were to have two-digit numbers prefixed with the letter N. Numbers 1–50 were reserved for national primary roads and 51–99 for national secondary roads. The numbers were allocated roughly following the pattern that had been used previously for the Trunk roads so that the new routes were numbered anti-clockwise out of Dublin, up to the N25 at that time, but up to the N32 by autumn 2001. Numbers N33 and N34 have also been allocated to new sections of road, but these numbers are an 'interim' solution pending further development of the network.

The national secondary numbers also ran roughly anti-clockwise around the country, starting with the N51 (up to the N83 at that time). However, although all these designations were used internally for grant purposes, the numbers did not appear on signposts and the T and L numbers continued in use.

Following the passing of the Local Government (Roads and Motorways) Act of 1974, legislation was passed (Statutory Instrument 167 of 1977) which enabled national road designation. The new system was thus introduced, which now used for all purposes the N prefixes for the main two classes of roads, that had already been used for internal purposes, whilst the M prefix was assigned to motorways. Motorway numbers tend to correspond with the designation of National roads, meaning that the M7 and N7 interchange, the M1 bypasses Balbriggan whilst the N1 passes through the town and so on. The N1/M1 pairing go north from Dublin towards Belfast and the N11/M11 combination leave south-east from the capital to Wexford.

## Regional Roads

In 1979, the Department issued a schedule and a map showing proposed regional roads and these were subsequently implemented both in respect of route number signposts and Ordnance Survey maps. The T and L numbers started disappearing at the same time, though many still exist today. Generally, T roads became N, and L roads became R. However, many longer T roads were broken into smaller R roads to give a more consistent layout and some L roads lost their classification altogether.

The regional roads are all allocated three-digit numbers in which the initial number (from 1–7 only) indicates the region of the country where the road is, as follows:

R101 – R149 Reserved for roads in, or starting in, the Dublin area.

R150 – R249 The North-east, Meath, Louth, Monaghan, Cavan.

R250 – R275 Donegal

R275 – R300 North-west, Sligo, Roscommon, Leitrim.

R301 – R390 West, Mayo, Galway.

R390 – R459 Midlands, Longford, Westmeath, Offaly, Laois, Kildare.

R460 – R525 Mid-west, Clare, Limerick, Tipperary N.R.

R550 – R650 South, Kerry, Cork.

R651 – R720 South-east, Tipperary S.R., Waterford, Kilkenny.

R720 – R799 East, Carlow, Wexford, Wicklow.

Gaps have been left in the sequences to provide for future development.

The other regional roads are in the main very short lengths within cities or other built-up areas and these are given numbers in the R8XX and R9XX series. These numbers therefore indicate that the roads are local intra-urban links, and because the roads are so short, their numbers are not shown on signposts or on Ordnance Survey maps. The numbering of these short roads also conforms to a pattern, as follows:

R801 – R845 Reserved for Dublin area (only 801–839 used initially).

R846 – R856 for Cork.

R857 – R859 for Limerick.

R860 – R862 for Waterford.

R863 – R866 for Galway.

– and continuing subsequently anti-clockwise around the country. The highest number used in 1994 was the R920.

A further Roads Act was passed in 1993, which led also to the setting up of a National Roads Authority. Statutory Instrument 209 of 1994 confirmed the previous statutes, but responsibility for the numbering system seems to have remained with the Road Policy Section of the Department of the Environment. The Minister now has powers to make any changes to the classification system, including those that might be brought in under European Union wide agreements.

## Local Roads

Before 1994, roads below the class of Regional were called 'Urban' if within the cities, boroughs or urban districts and 'County', if outside. Since 1994, however, they have all been termed 'Local', and divided into 'Local Primary', 'Local Secondary' and 'Local Tertiary' roads. These roads have all been given 4– and 5–digit numbers, such that each road in each county has a unique number. The size of all the road numbers throughout the whole country is also already an indication of a road's relative importance.

# TERMS USED IN THIS BOOK
## A roadmap to highway terminology

| | |
|---|---|
| ARTERIAL ROAD | Main road with no access from side streets, usually with dual carriageways and grade-separated junctions. Sometimes provided with service roads for access to property frontages. |
| BLACK TOP | Asphalt road surface. |
| CAUSEWAY | Historical term for a paved road. |
| DfT | Department for Transport |
| DISTRIBUTOR | The motorway equivalent of a service road, i.e. road running on either side of, and parallel to, a motorway, providing junctions to less important roads, generally in urban areas. |
| DIVIDED HIGHWAY | American term for dual carriageway. |
| DUAL CARRIAGEWAY | A road with a central reservation (British English) or median strip (American English) that divides the two traffic flows. |
| EXPRESSWAY, EXPRESS ROUTE | A major divided highway designed for high-speed travel, having few or no intersections (American usage). Known as a Motorway in British English. |
| FREEWAY | Synonym for Expressway. |
| GRADE-SEPARATED | An interchange or junction where traffic routes or flows avoid conflicting movements by means of flyovers. |
| GYTRATORY TRAFFIC SYSTEM | Original name for a roundabout. |
| H.M.S.O. | Her Majesty's Stationery Office |
| LIMITED ACCESS HIGHWAY | Synonym for Expressway. |
| MAGIC ROUNDABOUT | A two-way roundabout in which traffic can pass either side of a roundabout, joining and leaving at mini roundabouts. Notable examples exist in Swindon and Hemel Hempstead. |
| MINI ROUNDABOUT | A small roundabout used where space is limited. The circular island is painted on the road surface. |
| MoT | Ministry of Transport |
| MOTORWAY | A road reserved for motor traffic, usually but not always with separate carriageways for each direction of traffic. |
| ON RAMP, OFF RAMP | American English expression for the approach roads that allow traffic to join or leave a dual carriageway or motorway at junctions. |
| OS | Ordnance Survey. |
| PARKWAY | Sub-arterial route with special landscaping treatment to make it visually more attractive. |

| | |
|---|---|
| PAVEMENT | (British English) raised path at side of the road. (American English) metalled part of the road used by wheeled traffic. |
| PIKE | American abbreviation for turnpike. |
| PRE-MOTORWAY | A dual carriageway road built to near motorway standards. |
| ROAD BOOK | Road Books were published in Britain from the 17th to the 20th centuries. Distinct from atlases and map books, they were produced in two formats, one as text lists of places and with mileages along a particular travel route. The other style showed strip maps of the route in question, with prominence given to the homes of nobility, churches and some detail of the surrounding landscape. |
| RIBBON DEVELOPMENT | Uncontrolled growth alongside main roads outside urban areas. |
| ROUNDABOUT | A ring junction that obviates one traffic flow crossing the path of another. |
| SABRE | Society for All British Road Enthusiasts. |
| SEMI-MOTORWAY | A single carriageway road reserved for motor traffic. |
| SERVICE ROAD | A road running on either side of, and parallel to, a main road, providing access to roadside buildings, generally in urban areas. |
| SIDEWALK | American English term for pavement in British English. |
| SLIP ROAD | Approach road that allows traffic to join or leave a dual carriageway or motorway at junctions. |
| SUB-ARTERIAL ROUTE | A road of sufficient importance to warrant parallel service roads, roundabout junctions. |
| SUPERHIGHWAY | Synonym for expressway. |
| TERMINAL | Road junction at end of a trunk road or motorway. |
| THROUGHWAY, THRUWAY | Synonym for Expressway. |
| TRAFFIC CIRCLE | American English term for a roundabout. |
| TURNPIKE | Literally a pike (spiked barrier) that turns, in other words a revolving gate. In past times it came to mean the (conventional) gates set across a road to prevent passage until a toll had been paid, later by extension a turnpike road. In the USA it means an expressway on which tolls are collected. |
| TURNPIKE ROAD | Road on which tolls are payable. |
| WHITE TOP | Concrete road surface. |

# FURTHER READING

## Books and periodicals

- *ABC of British Roads*, by J.A. Hughes (Ian Allan Ltd), 1956.
- *Boys' Book of Roads*, by Charles Boff (George Routledge & Sons, Ltd), 1941.
- *British Road Numbering*, by J.C. Mann (Railway & Canal Historical Society – Road Transport Group – Occasional Paper Second Series No 21) March 1993.
- *British Road Numbering – Some Further Thoughts*, by Graham Bird (Railway & Canal Historical Society – Road Transport Group – Occasional Paper Second Series No. 45) September 1994.
- *C-roads on signposts and maps*, by Richard Oliver, in Sheetlines, Journal of the Charles Close Society, No.59, December 2000, pages 40–43.
- *Famous Roads of the World*, by E.F. Carter (Frederick Muller Limited) 1962.
- *Greater London Plan 1944*, by Prof. Patrick Abercrombie (His Majesty's Stationery Office) 1945.
- *New Roads for Britain*, by George C. Curnock (British Road Federation), 1944.
- *The King's Highway*, by Rees Jeffreys (The Batchworth Press), 1949
- *The Royal Road*, by Robert Allan (Sir Isaac Pitman & Sons Ltd), 1946.
- *War Plan UK*, by Duncan Campbell (Burnett Books), 1982.

## Internet

The following websites are packed with interesting information:

- Chris's British Road Directory http://www.cbrd.co.uk
- Euroroutes in the UK http://www.martynhicks.co.uk/personal/html/bristol/euroroutes.html
- European E road numbers
  http://everything2.com/index.pl?node_id=898477
  http://www.xs4all.nl/~eldonk/eroads
  http://www.elbruz.org/eroads/AGR_1.htm
  http://www.geocities.com/marcelmonterie/Ecomparison.htm
  http://www.reference.com/browse/wiki/International_E-road_network

- Major Roads of Great Britain http://euclid.colorado.edu/~rmg/roads
- Pre-motorway New Roads (arterial roads, suicide lanes and all that) http://speedlimit.dreamwater.org/newroads.html
- Society for All British Road Enthusiasts (SABRE) http://www.sabre-roads.org.uk
- The Motorway Archive http://www.ukmotorwayarchive.org
- UK Roads http://www.pberry.plus.com/ukroads
- UK Roads Portal http://www.uk-roads.org.uk/
- Wet Roads (guide to every UK ford, watersplash and tidal road) http://vamp.idlers.org/~jaffa
- World's road numbering systems http://monterie.homestead.com/files/index.htm

And in less serious vein –

- Motorway Steps (and where they may lead) http://www.motorway-steps.co.uk

# INDEX

Airstrips 79
Ancient trackways 8
Anomalies 66
Antonine Itineraries 10
Archaeology of new
    roads 72

Bibendum 22
Blackout 64, 78

C roads 37
Channel Islands 83
Class I and II roads 28
Class III roads 43
Cloverleaf junctions 41
County roads 37

D roads 37, 44
Daily Mail 29
Dartford Crossing 57
Defunct highways 71
Doubles 67

E roads 37, 74
Early times 8
East Lancashire Road
    47
Essential Service Routes
    77
Europe's busiest motor-
    way 58
Euroroutes 74

France 21

Great C Road Hunt 45
Greater London Plan 53
Guildford Bypass 24, 66

Henly's Corner 64
Highways Act 17
Hospital corridors 79

Ireland 85
Isle of Man 27, 80

Isle of Wight 81
Isles of Scilly 81

Kingston Bypass 59

Local Government Act
    46
London-Birmingham
    Motorway 48
London-Yorkshire
    Motorway 48
London Orbital
    Motorway 53

Macadam 15
Medway Towns Motor
    Road 48
Memorandum on
    Numbering Roads 20
Metcalf 15
Michelin Tyre Company
    21
Mickleham Bypass 47
Middle Ages 11
Military roads 79
Milton Keynes grid 73
Ministry of Transport
    19
Misfits 68
Missing numbers and
    junctions 69
MoT road map 27
Motorway Box 55
Motorway numbering
    49
Motorways 47

North Circular Road 53
North Orbital Road 53

Ordnance Survey 25
Orkney Islands 82
Outer Hebrides 82

Preston Bypass 48

Records 68
Red Flag Act 17
Rest houses 48
Reused numbers 66
Road Board 18
Road signs 27
Roman roads 9
Royal Aircraft
    Establishment 70
Ringways 55

Secret junctions 70
Sectors 24
Shetland Islands 82
Silvertown Way 42
South Circular Road 53
Special Roads Act 48
Splits 66
Statute of Winchester
    11
Stirling Corner 68
Suicide lanes 59
Swaps 66

Taplow 79
Telford 15
Terminology 90
Thanet Way 59
Toll Trusts 15
Trunk roads 38
Turnpike Acts 14

U roads 44
Unclassified roads 40
Useless motorways 59

Wade's Roads 16
Western Avenue 47
Western Isles 82

X roads 44